Murder Most Vile
Volume Eighteen
18 Truly Shocking
Murder Cases

Robert Keller

Please Leave Your Review of This Book At
http://bit.ly/kellerbooks

ISBN-13: 978-1978241176
ISBN-10: 1978241178

© 2017 by Robert Keller

robertkellerauthor.com

Table of Contents

Flesh and Blood

It is a highly controversial case, one that continues to provoke debate decades after a young mother was sent to death row for the savage murders of her children. Did Darlie Routier really take a butcher's knife and plunge it repeatedly into the chests of 6-year-old Devon and 5-year-old Damon? The evidence suggests that she did and that she was rightly condemned to death for her terrible crime. And yet, there are still those who believe in Darlie's innocence, pointing to evidence that the police overlooked during the original investigation. Why, for example, did investigators ignore a bloody fingerprint left on a kitchen counter? Why did they dismiss a bloodstained sock found 75 yards from the crime scene on a trajectory that a fleeing intruder might have taken? Why did they fail to consider the bruises on the young woman's arms? The truth is that we don't know the answers to these questions. We know only that two little boys were savagely slain and that there is more than enough evidence to support the notion that their mother was responsible. Or maybe not. You decide.

"911, what is your emergency?"

Doris Trammell, the night dispatcher for the Rowlett Police Department, had enjoyed a relatively peaceful shift. That was not unusual. The city of Rowlett, an upscale enclave to the northeast of Dallas, Texas, is a quiet place. Serious crime is a rarity here, or at least it was until that 911 call came in during the early hours of Thursday, June 6, 1996. The caller was a woman and she was hysterical.

"Somebody broke into my house! They stabbed me and my children!"

Trammell, of course, had been trained to deal with these situations. She glanced briefly at her computer clock which read 2:31 a.m. Then she punched the main police line and instructed units to standby for an emergency involving women and children. She then returned to her caller, entreating the woman to calm down and provide her name and address. The caller, however, wasn't listening. "My boys," she wailed. "Oh my God, my babies are dying!"

"Ma'am, please calm down and tell me what happened," the dispatcher repeated, keeping her eye on her computer screen as the caller ID software performed its magic. In the next moment a name and address popped up. Darin and Darlie Routier, 5801 Eagle Drive, Dalrock Heights. Trammell knew the area well. It was probably the most affluent neighborhood in town. She immediately passed the address on to emergency responders, sending an ambulance and police officers racing to the scene. The first to arrive was patrolman David Waddell and he knew immediately that this was something big.

Waddell had barely entered the residence when he encountered a woman in a blood spattered nightgown, sobbing hysterically and babbling something he couldn't understand. Looking past her into the lounge he saw what appeared to be the bodies of two small children, lying on the carpet, their clothes soaked with fresh blood. Officer Waddell rushed towards them, fell to his knees and quickly established that one of the boys had stopped breathing, while the other was drawing harsh, gurgling breaths. Judging by the amount of blood, both had been seriously injured. Waddell had a call to make and he made it instinctively. Instructing the mother to fetch towels to staunch the wounds, he began giving CPR to the boy who had stopped breathing. The mother, meanwhile, continued yelling, saying that the intruder had fled into the garage and might still be in the house. She ignored all instructions given by Waddell.

But Waddell, at least, had help by now. Police Sergeant Matthew Walling had arrived, along with paramedics Jack Kolbye and Brian Koschak. The EMTs immediately got to work, attempting to stop the bleeding and resuscitate the children. While they were so engaged, Waddell and Walling went to investigate the householder's assertion that the assailant had fled into the garage. Following a trail of blood through the kitchen and an entertainment room, they entered the garage with their weapons drawn and threw on the light switch ready for anything. But the space was empty. If the attacker had fled this way, he'd managed to escape, possibly through a side window, where the screen had been slashed. Or perhaps he was elsewhere in the house. The officers conducted a room-by-room search but found no stranger in hiding. They then returned to the kitchen where they'd spotted the possible murder weapon, a bloodied butcher knife carelessly cast aside on a countertop. They noticed something else too, something curious. The counter top was liberally smeared with blood but the sink was spotless and appeared to have been recently rinsed out.

By now, other police officers and medical personnel had descended on the house. In the street outside, the sweep of blue and red police lights threw splashes of color while officers strung up crime scene tape to keep inquisitive neighbors at bay. Inside, Sgt. Walling had finally managed to calm the distraught mother, now identified as Mrs. Darlie Routier. And he'd been able to glean from her a version of what had happened. It was a story she'd repeat numerous times over the days that followed, sometimes with embellishments and conflicting details.

According to Mrs. Routier, she had been downstairs with her two older sons, having fallen asleep in front of the television. Her husband, Darin, was upstairs in the master bedroom with their youngest, 7-month-old Drake. She'd woken with a man pinning her to the couch and had immediately started fighting and screaming, causing the intruder to flee. She'd then given chase but had just reached the kitchen when she decided to go back and check on her sons. It was only then that she realized they'd been stabbed. By then, her screams had awakened her husband and he'd come running downstairs. But it was too late, the intruder had already fled, leaving the two boys grievously injured.

More than grievously, as it turned out. Each of the boys had suffered two vicious stab wounds to the chest, thrusts that had missed the heart but had shredded lungs and severed vital arteries. Devon, 6, was pronounced dead at the scene while his younger brother, Damon, was critical. He was rushed to Baylor Medical Center but it was too late. Damon Routier was dead on arrival.

Compared to the horrific injuries inflicted on her sons, Darlie Routier had gotten off lightly. She'd suffered a wound to her throat and another to her right arm. The cuts were relatively shallow, although the neck wound had come dangerously close to her carotid artery. After answering further questions about the night's events, she was taken to Baylor Center for treatment of her injuries. By now, the case had been assigned to veteran Homicide Detective Jimmy Patterson and his partner, Chris Frosch. Patterson soon had reason to suspect that the story told by Darlie Routier was somewhat shy of the truth.

It started with an anecdote relayed to him by Sgt. Welling shortly after he arrived at the house. "You're not going to believe what Mr. Routier said to me right before he left to go to the hospital," Welling said. "He turned to me and I swear to God he said, 'Golly, I guess this is the biggest thing Rowlett's ever had.' Can you believe that? Two of his children have just been slaughtered and the man is acting like the damn circus is in town!"

Patterson did indeed think that that was odd. But he'd also been in the job long enough to know that people respond differently in times of tragedy and crisis. Still that was only the first of the anomalies he'd encounter that night. The next was the slashed screen over the window in the garage. Mrs. Routier had suggested that the killer had entered and exited the home in this way but that just didn't stack up. The screen was of the type that could be easily clipped from its frame so why slash it? And what had been used to make the cut? It certainly wasn't the murder weapon since the killer had only gained access to that once he was inside the house. That meant he must have arrived carrying a knife. Why then use a different blade to commit the murders? Why leave it behind with potential fingerprints?

That wasn't all that bothered Patterson about the killer's supposed escape route. After committing the murders, he would have been covered in blood and would undoubtedly have deposited some of it on the wall and on the screen as he fled. And yet, the Crime Scene Unit had found not a trace. A K-9 team had also tried to pick up a trail starting from the killer's alleged exit and had come up empty. The only conclusion that Patterson could draw from that was that the killer had neither entered not exited through the garage. And if that was the case, how had he gotten in? There was no sign of forced entry.

Also perplexing was the blood evidence found at the scene. A trail of blood did indeed lead along the escape route that Darlie had described the killer taking. The problem was that there were no footprints other than those made by Darlie's bare feet. And then there were indications, found by the CSIs, that someone had cleaned up blood in the kitchen sink and also on a leather couch. Why?

None of this added up and neither did the issue of the dog. The Routiers had a pet Pomeranian who a neighbor described as "yappy and highly suspicious of strangers." Where, Patterson wondered, had this little guardian been when the intruder had entered the house? Why had he not raised the alarm and woken the Routiers? There was only one possible answer that Patterson could think of. There had been no intruder. Someone in the house had done this.

The following day, Patterson and Frosch showed up at the hospital to question Darlie Routier. This time she provided a more detailed description of what had happened and some of those details directly contradicted the statement she'd given previously. Earlier, she'd stated that it had been the weight of the man on top of her that had jarred her awake. Now she said that she'd awakened to Damon's cries of "Mommy! Mommy!" as he tugged on her nightshirt.

"I opened my eyes and felt a man get off me. I got up to chase after him. As I flipped on the light in the kitchen, I saw him open his hand and let the knife drop to the floor. Then he ran out through the garage. I went over and picked up the knife. I shouldn't have picked it up. I probably covered up his fingerprints. I shouldn't have picked it up.

"I looked over and saw my two babies with blood all over them. I didn't realize my own throat had been cut until I saw myself in a mirror. I screamed out to my husband."

Routier went on to describe the man who had attacked her, saying that he was of medium-to-tall height, dressed all in black and wearing a baseball cap. That description was of little use to Patterson. Far more interesting was the information he was able to glean from questioning the nursing staff at the hospital.

They told of a cold and distracted woman who showed no emotion even when visiting relatives broke down in tears. Several of the nurses also mentioned that Darlie appeared determined that everyone should know she'd handled the murder weapon. She mentioned it numerous times, admonishing herself for picking up the knife and thus erasing the killer's fingerprints with her own. That, of course, didn't amount to evidence but it was certainly suspicious.

And Darlie's odd behavior continued at her sons' funeral. Whereas other family members and even neighbors were distraught with grief, she appeared strangely unmoved. Her relatives put it down to the Xanax she'd been prescribed and perhaps they were right. Who could really understand the emotional state of a mother who'd suffered such a devastating loss. And anyway, while the police may have had their suspicions, where was the motive? What possible reason could Darlie Routier have had for killing her children? There were no insurance policies, no bitter custody dispute. By all accounts, Darlie doted on her boys. Perhaps her background might yield some clue. The police started delving.

Born in Altoona, Pennsylvania, on January 4, 1970, Darlie moved with her mother to Texas after her parents divorced and her mother married a man named Dennis Stahl. That marriage would also end in divorce but, by all accounts, Darlie had a happy childhood and blossomed into a pretty, blond-haired teen. She met her future husband, Darin Routier, while she was still in school and apparently it was love at first sight. They continued to correspond after Darin went away to college and picked up their relationship after he graduated. Shortly after, Darin was hired by a computer chip company in Dallas and Darlie moved there to be near him and soon landed a job with the same company. They were married in August of 1988.

The couple began their life together in an apartment in Garland. Darin, however, had bigger dreams than working for a boss and living in rented accommodations. A year later, he rented a house in Rowlett and started his own computer company, Testnec, operating it out of his garage. It was a risk but one that would soon pay handsome dividends. It needed to. Darlie had just discovered that she was pregnant.

The couple's first child, Devon, was born on June 14, 1989 and was followed by his brother, Damon on February 19, 1991. By then, Darin's company had grown to such an extent that he'd had to hire additional staff and rent office space. The money was rolling in and the Routiers indulged themselves by commissioning a two-story Georgian mansion in the upmarket suburb of Dalrock Heights on the shore of Lake Ray Hubbard. Darin also bought himself a 27-

foot cabin cruiser while the family cruised the streets in a shiny new Jaguar. Life, it seemed, could not get any better.

Darlie was by all accounts a good mother, doting on her children, making a big fuss of Christmas and Thanksgiving celebrations and throwing elaborate parties on their birthdays. But there was another side to her. Ever since her teens, friends and acquaintances had noticed a certain neediness. Darlie always had to be the center of attention and with the money now available to indulge her obsession she held little back. She spent a fortune on clothes and convinced Darin to pay for size EE breast implants, assets she put to use by wearing the skimpiest, most revealing outfits. Inevitably, this led to problems in her marriage with the couple sometimes arguing in public over Darlie's flirting. Not that Darin was an angel either. Rumors abounded that both he and Darlie were having affairs.

Unfortunately, in such an unhealthy situation it is always the children who are going to suffer. Neighbors complained that Damon and Devon, hardly past the toddler stage, were often left home alone. And more and more people were noticing that Darlie's patience with her sons had become wafer thin. It was therefore a surprise to friends and family when Darlie announced early in 1995 that she was pregnant again. The Routiers' third son, Drake, was born on October 18, 1995. His arrival only served to spin Darlie off into postpartum depression, characterized by extreme mood swings and frighteningly dark rages.

To make matters worse, 1995 was also the year that the couple's exorbitant spending started to catch up with them. Darin's company was doing well, with a gross income of $264,000 for the tax year. But it was hardly a match for the millionaire lifestyle the couple was living. Soon they were turning to credit to keep up appearances. Then Darin began dipping into his business coffers with the inevitable fallout. Creditors began asking for payment and Testnec had no money to settle up. An application to his bank for a bridging loan of $5,000 was declined.

While all of this was going on Darlie was battling her own demons, struggling to lose the weight she'd put on during her last pregnancy, waging a losing campaign against depression, frustrated by the reins being applied to her spendthrift habits. The situation got so bad that she began contemplating suicide. On May 3, 1996, she wrote in her diary: "Devon, Damon and Drake, I hope you will forgive me for what I am about to do. My life has been such a hard fight for a long time, and I just can't find the strength to keep fighting anymore. I love you three more than anything else in this world and I want all three of you to be healthy and happy and I don't want you to see a miserable person every time you look at me."

Darlie Routier would never follow through on the threat to take her own life. But a month after she'd penned that poignant note, two of the sons to whom she had addressed it would be dead.

Back at Rowlett Police Headquarters, Det. Patterson was still wrestling with the many questions surrounding the case. Some of those would soon be answered. First the medical examiner's report on Darlie's injuries was back. The cuts, according to the M.E. were "hesitation wounds" that is, they had been inflicted slowly and deliberately, with the person reflexively withdrawing the blade as soon as pain is experienced. This was quite different to the wounds the boys had suffered. There the knife had been forcefully plunged in, with intent to kill.

Then there were the various forensic reports, most notably those regarding the screen and the mysteriously clean kitchen sink. The sink had shown a clear response to Luminol, meaning that it had definitely been washed clean of blood before the police arrived. By whom and why? Patterson thought he knew the answer. He believed that Darlie had inflicted her neck wound over the sink and had then rinsed away all traces of blood.

The evidence regarding the damaged screen was even more conclusive. A set of knives found in the Routier residence had been subjected to forensic analysis and had returned some interesting results. On a breadknife, technicians found traces of metal and Teflon that were forensically matched to the screen. This knife then, had been used to make the cut. Were the police to believe that an intruder had removed the knife from a drawer, slashed the screen, and then returned the knife to its original place? No, it all went to back up Patterson's theory that the intruder story was a lie concocted by the real killer. On January 18, 1997, Darlie Routier was arrested for the murder of her two sons.

Routier was indicted on two counts of first degree murder on June 28, 1997, although the DA later opted to try her only for Damon's murder, keeping the other charge in reserve, in the event of an acquittal.

That, in truth, never seemed likely. Routier's version of events was in direct conflict with the forensic evidence and in cases like that juries generally lean towards the forensics. The best shot that the defense had was to dwell on the one thing to which the police did not have a definite answer, the fact that Darlie Routier had no motive.

Except that that wasn't exactly true. There was plenty of evidence that Darlie was the "self-centered, materialistic woman" that the prosecutor described her as; plenty of evidence that she had at times neglected her children and had on other occasions been openly hostile towards them. There was witness testimony, too, of her odd behavior on the night her children died, of her callous attitude and lack of grief. And that had continued at the boys' funeral and beyond. One particular incident had involved a bizarre birthday party that Darlie had hosted at her sons' gravesite, complete with cake and silly string. Darlie's friends and family might have believed she was innocent, her attorney might have tried to prove it, but in the end, the evidence said different. That, at least, was how the jury ruled.

But were they right? After the trial, two pieces of evidence emerged that might have resulted in a different outcome. One was a bloody fingerprint found on a counter top which did not come from either Darlie or Darin Routier; another was a child's sock, discovered in an alleyway 75 yards from the crime scene. It was found to contain traces of both Devon and Darin's blood.

These perplexing clues might well cast doubt on the original conviction but they have not been deemed sufficient to gain a new trial for Darlie Routier. She remains incarcerated at the Mountain View Unit in Gatesville, Texas, awaiting her date with the executioner.

The Case of the Vanishing Bride

When Eileen Spargo and George Turner met in Auckland, New Zealand in 1942, sparks instantly flew between them. The attraction on her part was easy to understand. Turner was tall and handsome, suave and sophisticated. He was from an aristocratic family that had made millions in the steel industry. Now, he was the sole survivor of that dynasty. His entire family had been wiped out by a German bomb during the blitz. That meant that he was soon to inherit both his father's fortune and his title. Adding further spice to the mix was Turner's wartime occupation. He was a spy, working for British intelligence.

Turner's feelings towards Eileen were perhaps more difficult to fathom. The 30-something worked as a factory supervisor and was recently divorced. She was financially secure but not wealthy, attractive but certainly no society beauty. Nonetheless, the handsome British peer appeared besotted with her. After a whirlwind romance, he proposed and Eileen could not accept quickly enough. The wedding date was set for July 1942 and the couple then planned to take a short honeymoon before traveling to Australia and then on to Britain to start their new life together.

Eileen was almost beside herself in the weeks leading up to the wedding. It took all of her willpower to maintain the secrecy that her fiancée insisted upon. He did, at least, allow her to inform her parents and closest friends of her upcoming betrothal but they too were asked to keep things under wraps. Turner had also instructed Eileen to liquidate her financial holdings, to sell the house she'd received as part of her divorce settlement and to withdraw all of her savings. She'd have no need of these things once she was Lady Turner.

Finally, the big day arrived and the couple tied the knot at the Pitt Street Methodist Church in Central Auckland with a tight-knit group of family and friends in attendance. It was here that Eileen's parents first got to meet their new son-in-law and they were as impressed with him as their daughter had been. George Turner was utterly charming. The Spargos' only regret was that the occasion could not be commemorated with the traditional wedding photographs. The groom forbade the taking of pictures "on security grounds." And he gave the same reason for the lack of a wedding reception. Instead, the newlyweds drove in their rented car to Eileen's parents' home for a private dinner. They later checked in at the nearby Helensville Hotel.

At around 11:45 that evening, Eileen Spargo's lawyer was roused from his bed by the jangling of a telephone. Eileen was on the line with urgent instructions, something she wanted taken care of first thing in the morning. She said that she wanted him to draw a check on her trust account for the total proceeds of her house sale, a sum of around $55,000. The check was to be made out to George Turner and deposited in an account she designated, also in Turner's name. The lawyer found both the request and the hour of the call to be unusual. Nonetheless, he complied with his client's wishes.

The following morning, George and Eileen checked out of their hotel room and drove to Titirangi, an upmarket suburb of Auckland. There they visited Eileen's friend, Celia Shepherd, so that Eileen could say goodbye before they departed for Australia. When they left that afternoon, Eileen informed her friend that they were going to take a drive through the Waitakere Ranges, a picturesque area of hills and dense tropical forest to the west of Auckland. They then departed. It was the last time that anyone, bar her husband, saw Eileen Spargo Turner alive.

A month passed during which none of Eileen's friends or family heard a word from her or her husband. And yet none of them were at all concerned. Turner had warned them in advance that his job sometimes required him to "go dark" and that he and Eileen would be incommunicado during those periods. Then, in August, Eileen's parents were delighted to receive a letter postmarked Sydney, Australia and signed "George and Eileen." In it, the couple stated that they were both well and would be sailing for England within days.

That was the last that the Spargos heard of their daughter until one dreadful day in early December when their son-in-law appeared unexpectedly on their doorstep. The Spargos were more than a little surprised to see him, since they believed him to be in England, along with Eileen. But that surprise soon morphed into anguish as Turner explained the reason for his visit. He said that he and Eileen had traveled from Australia aboard the ocean liner, Empress of India. However, somewhere in the mid-Atlantic, the liner had been torpedoed by a German U-boat and had sunk with all on board. Turner had been separated from Eileen in the chaos but he'd managed to scramble onto some floating wreckage and had later been picked up by a British warship and taken to England. He'd remained in the hospital recuperating from his wounds for weeks. Of Eileen, however, there was no trace. It appeared she'd gone down with the ship.

The elderly couple were understandably devastated at the news. Their only daughter was gone, lost at sea, cruelly taken at the happiest point of her life. For weeks they continued to grieve until William Spargo's curiosity got the better of him and he began searching for information on the ill-fated Empress of India. What he found, shocked him to the core. There had indeed been a liner by that name but she had last sailed more than thirty years earlier and had since been scrapped. The story that Turner had told was a lie. On Christmas Eve 1942, Bill Spargo took this information to the police and reported his daughter missing. He also took with him the letter he had received from Australia back in August.

The case of the missing bride was handed to Detective Bill Fell, one of the Auckland Criminal Investigation Bureau's most competent investigators. Fell was very much the classic, hard-boiled gumshoe in trench coat and fedora but he was also somewhat of a new age man. Early in his career, he'd attracted plenty of ribbing from his fellow detectives for enrolling on a secretarial course to learn shorthand and typing. There was a method to his madness, of course. Fell was able to take witness statements and type up case files way faster than any of his colleagues. That gave him more time on the streets, chasing down criminals.

Fell's first move in the Turner case was to get William Spargo to write to George Turner at the Sydney postal address he'd previously used. Then, he enlisted the help of his Australian colleagues to place the post box under surveillance. Sure enough the letter was collected by a man who then put it in an envelope and posted it back to Auckland, addressed to one George Horry.

Detective Fell was well acquainted with Horry. He was a habitual criminal who had served most of his adult life behind bars, usually on charges of fraud. Horry fancied the long con and his scams usually involved seducing women and then relieving them of their life's savings. He also enjoyed posing as a member of the British nobility.

Horry, of course, was easy to trace. Detectives simply followed the redirected letter to the front door of his house in Mt Albert. There, they conducted a search which soon turned up a number of incriminating items, including a hatbox belonging to Eileen Spargo and a suitcase containing her wedding dress. Horry was then taken into custody and transported to police headquarters. Subjected to hours of interrogation, he eventually cracked and admitted that he had posed as George Turner and that he'd married Eileen Spargo under false pretenses. However, he had a ready explanation for why he'd done it, another fantastical tale

that made his story about the Empress of India seem reasonable
by comparison.

According to Horry, Eileen had been in on the fake marriage from
the start. In fact, it had been her idea, he insisted. He went on to
explain that Eileen had wanted to run off with a married man and
move with him to the U.S. However, she didn't want to upset her
parents and so she had approached him with a proposal. She
would pay him $55,000 to pose as her fiancée, enter into a bogus
union and then deliver her to her lover. He had fulfilled his part of
the bargain and had left Eileen in the company of a man shortly
after they'd left Celia Shepherd's house. He hadn't seen her since,
he said. At far as he knew, she was living happily in the U.S. with
her lover.

It was a quite unbelievable story but no amount of badgering by
Fell and his team could get Horry to retract it. Much to Fell's
disgust, he was forced to let Horry go, although the habitual
criminal soon reverted to type and was arrested soon after on an
unrelated fraud charge and sent to prison for five years. In the
meantime, Fell had developed his own theory of what had
happened to Eileen Spargo. He believed that Horry had murdered
Eileen and buried her body somewhere in the Waitakere Ranges.
He therefore organized a series of massive searches in the hope of
turning up the corpse. But it was always a long shot. The area is
vast and densely forested and ultimately the searches came up
empty.

Fast forward nine years to 1951. Eileen Spargo had by now been
declared legally dead while George Horry had long since been

released from prison and was enjoying one of his rare periods of sustained freedom. In the interim, Bill Fell had been promoted to head of the Auckland CIB. And yet, one case still gnawed at him. He wanted more than ever to bring Horry to justice for killing Eileen Spargo.

Fell was also aware that the time to bring charges against Horry was rapidly running out. Although there is no statute of limitation on murder, witnesses move away, they get old and forgetful, they die. If he was ever going to bring charges against Horry, it had to be now.

And so, Fell approached the Auckland Crown Solicitor's office with what he had on Horry. It didn't amount to much. There was plenty of circumstantial evidence but nothing that could forensically link Horry to murder. If indeed a murder had been committed at all. The absence of a body was a huge problem for the prosecution, since the popular view of that era was that murder could not be proven without a corpse. (This is, of course, incorrect in legal terms but it was the jury that the prosecution needed to convince.)

Fortunately, prosecutor Vincent Meredith KC was on the same page as Fell. He ordered the arrest of George Horry and charged Horry with the murder of Eileen Spargo. The trial was set for August 6, 1951 at the Auckland Supreme Court. It would be characterized by a mammoth legal tussle between prosecutor Meredith and Horry's defense counsel, Alexander Turner.

Turner, predictably, honed in on the fact that no body had been found. "We have no proof that Eileen Horry is dead," he told the jury, "Let alone that she is dead by George Horry's hand." Meredith, in response, presented a compelling trail of circumstantial evidence which included Horry's constantly changing stories, the bogus letters, the wedding gown found in his house, and the $55,000 he'd drained from Eileen Spargo's trust account. He also offered a rebuttal to Turner's contention that there could be no murder conviction without a body. "In that case," he contended. "All a murderer would have to do to avoid justice is to destroy the evidence of his handiwork or hide it in a place where it can never be found."

And it was perhaps that final argument that won the day. After deliberating for just an hour and 55 minutes, the jury returned to find George Horry guilty of murder. He was sentenced to life imprisonment with hard labor, serving 26 years before his release in 1967. He died fourteen years later, having never revealed the location of Eileen Spargo's body. She remains missing to this day.

Taken

On the day that she died, 22-year-old Dru Sjodin had everything to live for. The pretty blonde was a graphic design student at the University of North Dakota, she had a close and loving bond with her family, and she was in a steady relationship with a young man who she cared about. On the day that she died, Dru Sjodin made a single, innocuous decision, one that would end up costing her life. There was a purse that she'd had her eye on for some time. After finishing her shift at the Victoria's Secret store at Columbia Mall in Grand Forks, North Dakota, she decided not to go directly home but to stop off and buy it. That decision put her directly in the path of a killer.

Alfonso Rodriguez had also come to the mall that day, although his purpose was not to shop but to hunt. A serial offender with a rap sheet peppered with sex crimes, Rodriguez had just recently been released from a 15-year stint at Oak Park Heights, Minnesota's high-security prison. He'd sworn that he'd go straight after this latest period of incarceration but such promises are easily made and just as easily broken by psychopaths. On the afternoon of

November 22, 2003, he'd slipped a knife into his waistband and
set off in his 2002 Mercury Sable for the Columbia Mall. There he'd
loitered in the parking lot, waiting for some unsuspecting woman
to chance along. It wasn't long before he spotted a likely victim, a
petite blond carrying a shopping bag and talking on a cellphone,
oblivious to her surroundings. It helped that she was gorgeous.
Yes, Rodriguez decided, this one would do nicely.

Dru's boyfriend, Chris Lang, had been talking on the phone to her
for a couple of minutes. He'd been asking when she expected to be
home and whether he might see her before she set off for her
waitressing job at the El Roco nightclub. Then suddenly, the call
was interrupted and he heard Dru say, "Oh my God!" and then "No,
no!"

"Dru?" Chris said. "What's going on?" But there was nothing but
silence. The line had gone dead. Chris then tried calling back but
the phone just rang, without being answered. Then followed a
frantic dash to the mall to try and find Dru and a call to her
roommate, Meg Murphy, to see if she'd made it home. Meg then
phoned El Roco to see if Dru had perhaps gone directly to work.
She hadn't. At around 7:40, Chris did eventually get a call from Dru
but there was only static on the line, plus the beep-beep-beep of
numbers being pressed at random. That call, it would later be
determined, had come from a rest stop near Crookston, Minnesota.
At 9:30 that evening, Chris and Meg went to the police and
reported Dru missing.

By the following morning, Dru Sjodin had been officially classified
as a missing person and the hunt to find her was underway. Police

officers descended in numbers on the Columbia Mall and soon located Dru's red, 1994 Oldsmobile Cutlass, still parked in the spot where she'd left it. Her pocketbook and a shopping bag containing the new purse were in the car but her keys and cell phone were missing. And there was another, potentially ominous, clue. The empty sheath of a hunting knife lay nearby. Had that perhaps have been dropped by the abductor in the process of subduing his victim? The police thought it might have. The mall's surveillance footage would tell them more.

In the meantime, news of Dru's disappearance had gone viral and the people of Grand Forks had responded en mass in their effort to help. Citizens banded together to form search parties, flyers were quickly printed and appeared overnight on light poles and in store fronts, someone had lapel pins made up, with a picture of Dru, and the message "Come Home." When Dru's parents put up a $20,000 reward for information, an anonymous benefactor matched that amount. The entire city appeared to be rooting for the missing girl, praying that she'd be found alive.

And the police were certainly leaving no stone unturned in their hunt for Dru Sjodin. Search teams comprising law officers and hundreds of civilian volunteers had spread out across the Grand Forks area. Other searchers had been dispatched to Crookston, Minnesota, where Dru's last cell phone signal had been picked up. Roadways, woods and the expanse of the Red Lake River were combed; ditches, fields and farmland were meticulously scanned. A helicopter was brought in and several teams of trained tracking dogs probed the most likely areas. Yet as the days stretched on, there was no trace of Dru. It was as if the earth had opened up and swallowed her.

Detectives meanwhile, had been working through the video footage from the Columbia Mall, trying to pick up some clue as to what had happened to the missing woman. And while they refused to disclose publically what they'd seen on the tapes, they soon had a line on a suspect, 50-year-old Alfonso Rodriguez, Jr. Rodriguez, of course, was no stranger to the police. He was a Level 3 sex offender, with a long history of violent sexual assaults against women. If it was indeed he who had taken Dru, then the police had reason to seriously fear for her safety. They therefore wasted little time in tracking him down to his home in Crookston. On December 1, 2003, one week after Dru Sjodin went missing, Rodriguez was taken into custody and charged with her kidnapping.

Rodriguez was subjected to a fierce round of interrogation by the Grand Forks police and also by the FBI, who had entered the case since kidnapping is a federal offense. But Rodriguez had danced this dance before. He was an old hand at the game. He steadfastly denied any involvement in Dru's disappearance and accused the police of "harassing an old con who was trying to get his life together." Those denials however, were contradicted by the evidence. The police had impounded Rodriguez's Mercury Sable, and had found bloodstains and a four-inch jackknife which was soaking in a plastic container filled with household detergent. The knife would later be matched to the sheath found in the vicinity of Dru's vehicle while the blood told an even more damning truth – it produced a DNA match to Dru Sjodin.

Based on the evidence now in their possession the police considered it highly unlikely that Dru would be found alive. But that did not mean that they had given up hope of finding her. Indeed, the search was about to reach a whole new level of intensity, when the governors of North Dakota and Minnesota called a press confidence on December 9, and announced that they were calling out the National Guard to join the hunt. Meanwhile, the man who could have brought the matter to a close in an instant was still refusing to cooperate with the police. Instead, he was agitating for bail. When it was eventually granted, the amount was fixed at a staggering $5 million. Rodriguez, in any case, had decided that he would prefer to remain behind bars. The mood against him was ugly. He feared for his safety.

The holiday season of 2003 was a muted affair in Grand Forks. It was as though a pall hung over the town and in particular over Dru Sjodin's family. They missed her smile and her infectious laugh, the ability she seemed to have to light up any room she walked into. The thought of her lying out there, out in the cold, was almost too much to bear. The police had by now informed them that the chances of finding Dru alive were highly unlikely. Still they yearned to have her home, to say their goodbyes and to lay her to rest. That, at least, would bring some sort of closure.

The search for Dru had by now expanded to an area covering roughly 30-square-miles and stretching from Grand Forks into Minnesota. Yet, as 2003 became 2004, as winter loosened its grip and gave way to the first signs of spring, Dru Sjodin remained among the missing. At least the snow was melting. That at least gave the searchers hope that their five-month quest would soon be resolved.

On April 17, 2004, a police reservist and a retired deputy were searching an area near the Minakwa Golf Club, to the west of Crookston. One of the men spotted the edge of a blanket, pushing through the snow in a shallow ravine. He scrambled down the bank to check it out and made a gruesome discovery. It contained the well-preserved but horribly mutilated remains of a young woman. Dru Sjodin had been found. An autopsy would later reveal the full extent of her horrible end. She had been subjected to sexual torture and extreme physical abuse before her killer ended her life at the end of his blade. Death, when it came, must have seemed like a blessing.

Dru Sjodin was laid to rest at the Pinewood Cemetery in Crosslake on April 24, 2004. Earlier, over 1,500 mourners had attended her funeral service at Grand View Lodge near Nisswa, Minnesota, all of them deeply touched by a moving eulogy that had described Dru as a "young woman with a generous heart and an infectious spirit."

In the meantime, the man who was the very antithesis of that sentiment, languished in a Grand Forks police cell, still unrepentant, still denying responsibility. It would be over two years before Alfonso Rodriguez Jr was brought to trial, the delays caused mainly by jurisdictional issues. Rodriguez must have thought that, because North Dakota had abolished the death penalty in 1975, he was looking at another prison term, something that held little fear for him. But he'd committed a federal offense by kidnapping Dru, transporting her across state lines and then killing her. Moreover, it was an offense that carried the possibility of death by lethal injection. When Rodriguez appeared at the Quentin Burdick Federal Courthouse on July 6, 2006, U.S. Attorney

Drew Wrigley made it clear that the federal government would indeed be seeking the death penalty.

On September 22, 2006, Alfonso Rodriguez was found guilty of kidnapping and murder and sentenced to death, a decision that was criticized by human rights groups but applauded elsewhere. He currently awaits execution.

FOOTNOTE: On July 27, 2006, President George W. Bush signed into law the Child Protection and Safety Act. This includes Dru's Law, which saw the establishment of the National Sex Offender Public Website. This resource provides information to the public on the whereabouts of registered sex offenders.

A Family of Killers

In the early months of 1987, a school located in Kiev, Ukraine suffered a double tragedy. Two staff members died in quick succession, both with similar, inexplicable symptoms. The first of these was the school "Partorg" (a role that encompassed responsibility for ideological education as well as human resources); the second was the institution's "nutrition nurse," a woman in her twenties, who had appeared to be in good physical health. Doctors who examined the two were baffled by their symptoms, which included chronic joint pain and almost complete hair loss. Unable to determine the cause behind these afflictions, they fell back on the diagnosis prevalent in Soviet medicine at that time. According to their death certificates, both victims had died of heart failure.

A short while later, on an afternoon in March of 1987, a Kiev hospital was suddenly inundated with a rash of emergency admissions. Several desperately ill children arrived almost simultaneous at the facility, all of them writhing in agony. The youngsters had been picked up at various locations, although a common link was soon established. They all attended the same school. Then, as doctors fought desperately to stabilize their young patients, a call came in from the school itself. Two adults – a teacher and a refrigerator repair man – had been struck down by the same mystery ailment. An ambulance was immediately dispatched to bring them to the hospital. Within 24 hours, both adults, as well as two of the 11 children admitted on that horrific day, had died in agony.

A link was quickly established between those deaths and the two that had occurred earlier in the year at the same school. The question was, what had caused them?

Initially, it was speculated that some sort of infection was responsible. However, the symptoms displayed by the patients were inconsistent with this. None, for example, had shown any evidence of fever.

Then, it was thought the victims had been exposed to some sort of poison or radioactive material. The Chernobyl nuclear disaster had occurred less than a year prior. Had radioactive material somehow made it to this Kiev school? Not wanting to take any chances, hospital administrators contacted the Sanitation and Epidemics Station (Russia's version of the CDC). It wasn't long before SES technicians in protective suits were wandering the halls of the school with Geiger counters. The results, however, showed no signs of contamination.

Meanwhile, back at the hospital, the bloodwork of all the patients, including the four who had died, was back. And the doctors were in for a surprise - all had tested positive for the poison, thallium. Tests were then ordered on the exhumed corpses of the two earlier victims and returned a similar result.

With the discovery of thallium in the bodies, the symptoms made perfect sense. But while that question was now answered, another was raised. How had the victims come into contact with the deadly substance? SES officials suspected accidental exposure, perhaps as a result of careless pest control measures. The school building was thus subjected to a thorough sweep. No trace of the poison was found.

That left only one explanation for the six deaths - deliberate poisoning. What had started out as the suspected leak of radioactive materials was now a homicide investigation.

As detectives descended on the school and began questioning faculty and learners, their suspicions fell initially on a talented middle-grader who was said to be obsessed with chemistry. The boy had once played a prank on the gym teacher, coating his whistle with a mildly corrosive substance that had caused the man's lips to blister. However, the youngster had no possible way of obtaining thallium and in any case had no motive for poisoning any of the victims. Besides, another of those afflicted was the school chemistry teacher, with whom the boy had a good relationship. That teacher had survived, despite suffering debilitating symptoms. Under questioning, he provided investigators with an interesting snippet of information. In addition to his role in the chemistry department, he was also responsible for the school's food inventory.

That clue set alarm bells jangling with detectives. Suddenly the connection they'd been missing appeared crystal clear. All of the deaths were somehow connected to the school kitchen. The nutrition nurse; the Partorg who oversaw all of the school workers, including the kitchen staff; the chemistry teacher, who was responsible for food inventory; the technician who had been called in to fix the school's broken refrigerator the day he fell ill; the metal shop teacher who had assisted him in the job; the children who had all eaten in the cafeteria. If there was a mass poisoner, investigators decided, he or she was to be found working in the kitchen.

The detectives' first step before interrogating the kitchen staff was to speak to the SES workers who had carried out the Geiger sweep of the school. Had they noticed anything unusual while processing the kitchen area? Several of them had. A dishwasher, Tamara Ivanyutina, had made a nuisance of herself during the procedure, following the technicians around, constantly under their feet even after the area had been cordoned off. She'd been asked to leave several times and eventually had been removed forcibly after she became insolent and abusive.

While all of this was going on, a second team of detectives was working the investigation from a different angle, making the rounds of various geological labs in Kiev, trying to trace the source of the thallium. It wasn't long before they hit pay-dirt. After finding a discrepancy in the inventory at one facility, they began interrogating lab technicians and soon extracted a tearful confession from one of them. The young woman said that she had given about 50 milligrams of Clerici solution to a friend of hers, something she'd been doing regularly since 1976. The friend had told her that her parents required it for pest control. Pressed for the friend's name, the young lab tech said that it was Nina Maslenko. Nina, as it turned out, was the sister of Tamara Ivanyutina.

Tamara Maslenko (later Ivanyutina) was born in Tyumen, Siberia in 1942. Her parents, Anton and Maria, had been relocated there from war-torn Ukraine during WWII. They would spend several years in the unwelcoming backwater before returning eventually to Kiev, via the Ukrainian towns of Kherson and Tula. It was a decades-long sojourn, during which the couple had six children. They arrived back in Kiev in the early 80s to take up residence in a crumbling ruin of a building, where they shared an apartment with several other families. By then, four of their offspring had cut all ties with the family. It is not difficult to understand why.

Anton and Maria Maslenko appear to have been a particularly malevolent couple, who sought to instill in their children an ideology based on hatred and self-interest. Succeed at any cost and crush those who stand in your way; trust no one and let no slight go unpunished. This was their ethos, one that their remaining children, Nina and Tamara, readily bought into.

And that philosophy was more than just theoretical. Crammed into their overcrowded apartment, the Maslenkos were soon involved in disputes and squabbles with their neighbors. Those who made enemies of them, invariably, were not long for this world. One man was poisoned because his TV was too loud; a woman was killed after making an ill-advised remark about the squalid condition of the Maslenkos' living area. Then Nina entered into a marriage of convenience with a much older man and he died within days of the wedding, leaving her a spacious apartment in the Kiev city center. She then seduced a younger beau but began poisoning him after he refused to marry her. The man survived but was left incapacitated and impotent.

Neither were these the first victims of the Maslenko clan. Anton is believed to have committed his first murder as far back as the 1930s. He would later admit to poisoning a female relative in the Seventies. The woman had had the temerity to suggest that he should prepare himself for the worst after Maria was hospitalized with a serious illness. "She dared imagine the death of my beloved wife," Maslenko would later confess, "so I killed her."

What is perhaps most shocking about these murders, is the casual indifference with which they were committed. Yet for all of the psychopathic exploits of her parents and sister, Tamara was the worst of the bunch.

The first murder that can be definitely attributed to Tamara was that of her husband, a truck driver who she'd married in haste and thereafter decided was below her station. Seeking a way out, Tamara had given no thought to divorce. Why concern yourself with such trivialities when there was a supply of thallium at the ready? The truck driver had departed on a road trip carrying a batch of sandwiches prepared by his wife and had never returned.

Thereafter, Tamara had set her sights on a recent divorcee, seven years her junior.

Oleg Ivanyutina was instantly attracted to the pretty but overweight Tamara. It is easy too, to see what attracted her to him. His parents had a free standing house with a large backyard on the outskirts of Kiev. Tamara, who had ambitions of raising livestock and operating a butcher shop, undoubtedly had her eye on that property.

But it was soon clear that the elder Ivanyutins did not like Tamara. In truth, she was a difficult person to like – combative, rude and obnoxious, interested in nothing other than getting her own way. The Ivanyutins were keen on a grandchild, which Tamara, by now in her early forties, seemed incapable of producing. When they suggested adoption, Tamara balked. Eventually, frustrated with the situation, they gave Oleg and Tamara an ultimatum. They had a year to produce a grandchild, by whatever means. Failing that, the Ivanyutins would write Oleg out of their will and bequeath their house to some distant relative.

It was an ill-advised threat, one that amounted to a death sentence for those issuing it.

Oleg's father was the first to die. He fell ill soon after eating a meal prepared by his daughter-in-law. His wife followed him to the grave just a few weeks after the funeral, having suffered many of the same symptoms – joint pain, abdominal cramps, hair loss, and ultimately heart failure. Despite symptoms that seemed to suggest otherwise, both deaths were put down to coronary problems.

With her in-laws out of the way, Tamara finally had her hands on a property big enough to realize her dream. Shortly thereafter, she began raising pigs. By all accounts, she was a good farmer, her animals fat and healthy. Her husband, meanwhile, appeared to have contracted the same disease that had taken his parents. He began steadily losing weight, lost all of his hair, and began suffering severe pains in his joints. Barely into his mid-thirties he looked twice that age and could only walk doubled over and supported by a cane.

Despite her burgeoning business, Tamara continued to work at her lowly job as a dishwasher in the school cafeteria. The reason for this was simple. Keeping livestock was an expensive undertaking and she lacked the funds to buy feed for her pigs. Working in the cafeteria gave her access to untold quantities of food that she could pilfer and carry home. She was hardly subtle about it either. She stole without any attempt at subterfuge. Almost daily, she'd be seen leaving the school premises carrying large, heavy bags.

Often, she'd be seen stalking the cafeteria floor chasing slow eaters from their meals which she'd then scoop up into one of her bags. On one occasion, two young children – a first-grader and a fifth-grader – approached the cook for some scraps to take home to their pet. Tamara was furious. She waited for the children outside and angrily demanded that they hand the food over to her. Within days of that incident both of the children became seriously ill, suffering joint pain and hair loss. They would remain so for over a year as Tamara continued to feed them small doses of poison, not enough to kill but certainly enough to keep them in agony. Even against children, she held a grudge for a long time.

But Tamara's wholesale thievery had not gone unnoticed. The school's nutrition nurse had eventually had enough and confronted her, instructing her to stay away from the refrigerators and the stoves and to stop harassing the children. When Tamara ignored this instruction, the nurse went to the chemistry teacher responsible for food inventory and he, in turn, reported the matter to the school Partorg. Tamara was hauled before the local Communist Party Committee, where she suffered a humiliating dressing-down before being released with a warning. Not long after, the nurse and the Partorg became ill and ultimately died. The chemistry teacher suffered similar symptoms but survived.

With her accusers dispatched, Tamara decided on a new ploy. She sabotaged the cafeteria's refrigeration units, hoping that the food would spoil and that she'd then be allowed to take it home to her pigs. But the school was quick to attend to the problem, summoning a repairman that same day. Tamara then poisoned a pot of buckwheat soup that she knew would be given to the repairman for his lunch. The twelve children that were also poisoned, she considered collateral damage. She had never liked children anyway.

But the mass poisoning had been a major miscalculation on her part. With evidence of thallium in the bloodwork of the victims and eyewitness testimony as to her strange behavior, Tamara was placed under arrest. When a vial of Clerici solution was discovered at her house, the game was finally up for the serial poisoner.

With Tamara now in custody, attention turned to her parents. The police, however, had very little evidence against them at this point, aside from the fact that they had procured the thallium. But then Maria Maslenko made it easy for them. She tried to kill a neighbor with a batch of poisoned pancakes (the woman's only offense appeared to be that Maria was jealous of her war veteran's pension). Fortunately, the woman was suspicious of Maria's sudden show of generosity and rather than eat the pancakes she packed them up and took them to the police. Tests would prove that they were tainted with enough thallium to kill several times over.

All four members of the murderous Maslenko clan would eventually be tried for murder. Nina would face only one charge, for killing her elderly husband. She was sentenced to the relatively light term of 16 years for the crime. Anton and Maria Maslenko were also convicted. Their sentences of thirteen and ten years respectively would amount to life in prison, as both died behind bars.

As for the primary focus of the murder inquiry, Tamara Ivanyutina was found guilty on multiple counts and sentenced to death. The Soviet state was not in the habit of making public statements about executions but it is believed that she was put to death by a bullet to the back of the head sometime in the late eighties. She would be the last woman executed in the Soviet Union.

Subsequent to the execution, investigators began looking into suspicious deaths in other places where the Maslenkos had lived before arriving back in Kiev. In each of those cities, they found numerous unexplained deaths directly connected to the family, although no further charges were ever brought.

Germ Warfare

Arthur Warren Waite was born in 1889 in rural Michigan. His parents were dirt poor sharecroppers and Arthur grew up lacking everything in life but the bare necessities. As a child, he suffered a bout of meningitis which few expected him to survive. Yet he not only overcame the illness but thrived in its aftermath. Those who knew him from that time, said that Arthur's personality changed after that episode. Whereas before he'd been shy and reticent, he now became outgoing and gregarious; where he'd been a mediocre student, he went on to graduate near the top of his high school class. When he was accepted into dentistry school after graduation, it appeared that the poor farmer's son from Michigan was on his way up.

But there were other aspects to the new and improved Arthur Waite that were not as positive. Friends noticed a tendency to manipulate people and situations for his own benefit, a coldness of purpose, a lack of empathy. By now a tall and handsome young man, Arthur appeared to enjoy toying with the affections of the many women attracted to him, he seemed to think nothing of lying and cheating, indeed he seemed to revel in dishonesty. Had those friends been better informed, they might have recognized Arthur's behavior as that of a budding psychopath.

In 1908, while still enrolled in dentistry school, Waite began dating a young woman named Clara Peck. His friends were somewhat perplexed by the match, since the homely Clara was unlike the attractive debutantes that Waite typically pursued. Waite, however, wasn't interested in Clara for her looks. Her father, John E. Peck, was a self-made millionaire who'd built his fortune in the lumber industry. The Pecks counted themselves among the social elite of Grand Rapids, Michigan. Waite wanted a part of that life and lifestyle. To him, Clara Peck was little more than a key to unlock the door.

And so Waite got to work on the Peck family. John Peck was at first suspicious of the young man's intentions but he was powerless against the charm offensive that Waite launched. Waite was charming and urbane, attentive to Clara, courteous to her family, heavy on the compliments. He soon convinced John Peck of his good intentions then won over the rest of the clan. The only dissenter was Clara's brother, Percy, who was convinced that Waite was working an angle. And Percy was right. The first part of Waite's plan was to get the family's blessing for a marriage to Clara.

Before that could happen, however, disaster struck for Waite. He was caught plagiarizing another student's work and was threatened with expulsion from the dentistry school. Rather than suffer that ignonimity, he quit. But that left him with a problem.

How was he going to explain to Clara's family that he'd dropped out when he'd already regaled them with his grandiose plans of setting up a dental practice in New York? The solution that he came up with was typical Waite.

Shortly after quitting school, Waite arrived one day at the Peck mansion in a state of great excitement. He produced a letter, supposedly from Glasgow University in Scotland, which offered him the opportunity to study at that institution's renowned dentistry school. This, he informed Clara, was the chance of a lifetime, one that he couldn't possibly pass up. It meant, however, that they'd have to put their marriage plans on hold while he completed his studies abroad. Eventually, over tearful protests, Clara agreed.

The letter that Waite had presented was, of course, a fraud. There had been no invitation from Glasgow University. Nonetheless, Waite traveled to Scotland and obtained admission to the postgraduate program using fake diplomas and letters or recommendation. He'd ultimately graduate with a master's degree. Thereafter, he decamped to South Africa where he worked for two years as the company dentist for a gold mining company. He was eventually fired over a large sum of money that went missing from a safe. Thereafter, he returned to Michigan where Clara was still patiently waiting.

Back in the States, Waite wasted little time in pressing ahead with marriage plans. After the wedding, the couple settled down to life in a luxury brownstone at 435 Riverside Drive on Manhattan's Upper Westside, a wedding gift from John Peck. Waite also set up a dental practice but, in truth, he had little enthusiasm for his chosen profession. He spent most of his time playing tennis and carrying on a torrid affair with society beauty Margaret Horton, wife of a prominent New York businessman.

Waite did, however, retain some interest in medical matters. In 1915, he enrolled as a private student at Cornell Medical School. His interest was in bacteriology, a strange field perhaps for a dentist but not one that raised any red flags, since private study was not as strictly managed as regular student enrollments. Thus, Waite presented his fraudulently-gained master's diploma and was allowed to start working with some of the deadliest pathogens available, typhoid, cholera, diphtheria, tuberculosis, and anthrax among them.

Most doctors who embark on the study of lethal micro-organisms do so for the purpose of curing and preventing disease. But Dr. Waite's motivation was far less altruistic. He had decided that it was time to move ahead with the next part of his plan, a plan that involved removing all obstacles standing between him and the Peck fortune. Ideally, he'd have waited a year or two, so as not to arouse suspicion but the matter had been taken out of his hands just months into his marriage to Clara. His in-laws had begun to have second thoughts about the union and to question Waite's work ethic and general integrity.

Just after Christmas 1915, Clara's mother came to spend a couple of weeks with her daughter at the Riverside Drive condominium. She'd been there barely a day when she had to be confined to bed with a bad cold. It was hardly a life-threatening illness but Dr.

Waite immediately declared that he would dedicate himself to his mother-in-law's recovery. And he attacked that task with vigor, supervising Mrs. Peck's meals, massaging her feet, mopping her brow, even singing to her in his tuneful tenor voice. He also treated her with a special nasal spray of his own design, assuring her that it would facilitate a swift recovery. In fact, it contained a deadly blend of diphtheria and anthrax. Then, as the unfortunate woman's condition worsened, Waite sped her on her way by dampening her sheets with cold water and leaving the windows wide open in the midst of a New York winter. Mrs. Peck died on January 30, 1916. Her death was attributed to "natural causes."

John Peck was devastated by the unexpected loss of his beloved wife, while Percy and Clara were similarly distraught. It is therefore fortunate that Dr. Waite was there to take charge of the funeral arrangements. His main concern was for the remains to be cremated as swiftly as possible. This, he assured the undertaker, was to spare the family "unnecessary anguish."

About two months after the death of his wife, John Peck himself fell ill, a condition many attributed to his grief. What no one (not even the ultra-suspicious Percy) suspected, was that the illness was induced rather than natural. Waite had moved on to the next part of his plan.

Peck, however, would prove a rather tougher individual than his deceased wife. Waite put ground glass in his food, released chlorine gas in his bedroom, doped him with the fungicide calomel. He exposed his father-in-law to a catalog of deadly pathogens, including tuberculosis, anthrax and diphtheria. He soaked his bedsheets and left windows open to induce pneumonia. When none of these measures delivered the desired effect, he fed the man 18 grams of arsenic, a dose that should have been fatal. All Peck suffered was a stomach upset and abdominal pain.

Waite's patience was by now wearing thin, driving him to ever more desperate measures. Eventually, he abandoned all attempts at subtlety and placed a chloroform-soaked rag over his father-in-law's mouth and nose. Then he positioned a pillow over the old man's face and pressed down until Peck stopped breathing.

It had taken Waite six weeks to dispose of his father-in-law. Now he followed his familiar path, generously offering to take care of the funeral arrangements. This time, however, Percy Peck was less inclined to accede to the request. Waite's eagerness bothered him. What, he wondered, was his brother-in-law hiding? The answer came on the day of John Peck's memorial service, a tersely worded letter consisting of just six words: "Stop funeral. Demand autopsy. Suspicions aroused." It was signed "K. Adams."

Percy, as we have already noted, had never been Arthur Waite's biggest fan. He took the letter to his local precinct where he handed it over to a homicide detective, explaining that both of his parents had died unexpectedly within the space of two months. Officers were then sent to Waite's dental practice to question him. The dentist, however, had somehow got wind of Percy's visit to the police and had swallowed a handful of Veronal tablets in an apparent suicide attempt. He may well have died had the officers not arrived when they did.

Waite was rushed to Bellevue Hospital where he would eventually make a full recovery. In the meanwhile, an autopsy was carried out on John Peck's body and turned up copious amounts of arsenic. Vials of the same poison had been found hidden at Waite's practice making him the obvious suspect. His impetuous nature had cost him dearly. Had he stuck to naturally occurring pathogens, he might well have escaped detection. As it was, he found himself arrested and charged with two counts of capital murder.

As the matter headed towards trial, Waite must have known that the cards were stacked significantly against him. There was plenty of evidence to support capital murder charges and guilty verdicts on those charges would send him to the electric chair. He therefore resorted to a strategy employed by murderous felons through the ages. He decided to plead insanity.

Waite's first attempt at creating grounds for a diminished responsibility plea was so ludicrous it was embarrassing. He claimed that he was possessed by the spirit of a long dead Egyptian Pharaoh. "Although my body lives in America," he told incredulous detectives, "My soul lives in Egypt. It is the man from Egypt who has committed these foul deeds." The officers all but laughed him out of the interrogation room.

Then Waite tried another approach. He decided to tell all, but to deliver his confession in such a jovial way that his interrogators must take him for a madman. And so he spilled the beans, describing his horrific deeds in such graphic detail that hardened detectives occasionally flinched. What made it even more disconcerting was the constant smile he wore on his lips, the insane chuckle he punctuated his speech with. Surely someone who could adopt this attitude while talking about putting someone to a slow and painful death had to be insane? Waite even went on to admit that the senior Pecks had not been his only victims. He'd also tried to poison Clara and her aunt Catherine. Speaking of Clara, he cold-heartedly quipped: "She was not my equal in anything. Once I was rid of her I planned to find myself a more beautiful wife."

Arthur Warren Waite was brought to trial in New York in May 1916. Since he openly admitted his guilt, the main issue for the court was to decide the issue of his sanity. But here, Waite had been his own worst enemy. After his arrest, he'd written a letter to his lover, Margaret Horton, in which he'd told her that the only way he could avoid the electric chair was to feign insanity. Horton had since destroyed the letter but her testimony in court was enough to convince the jury. Waite's insanity defense was out the window. He was found guilty and sentenced to death.

Few killers in New York's history can have more richly deserved their date with Ol' Sparky, the electric chair at Sing Sing Prison. But to Waite's credit, he went to his end with a modicum of dignity. When the execution party arrived at his cell on May 24, 1917, they found the convicted killer reading from the works of his favorite poet, John Keats. He was then led to the execution chamber, remaining entirely calm as the straps were tightened and the electrodes fixed to his body. "Is this all there is to it?" he asked as the guards stepped back from their handiwork. Then two massive jolts of electricity were passed through his body. He was certified dead soon after.

Friday the 13th

There are some crimes whose impact is not softened by the passage of time, some murders that continue to haunt our thoughts and dreams even decades after they were committed. Most often, these are the crimes involving the most innocent victims of all, the slaughter of helpless children. And yet, even in the dreadful pantheon of child killers, of monsters like Westley Alan Dodd and Amelia Dyer and Tsutomu Miyazaki, the name of David McGreavy holds a special revulsion. The murders he committed are among the most bestial you are ever likely to read about.

David Anthony McGreavy was born in Southport, some 17 miles north of Liverpool, England, in 1951. His father, Thomas, was a sergeant in the Royal Signals unit and David, along with his five siblings, spent most of his upbringing moving from one army base to another, both within the UK and abroad. Notwithstanding these upheavals, his childhood was by all accounts normal, even if he appears to have grown into a somewhat conceited and occasionally dishonest teenager.

David's dream was to follow his father into the military and in 1967, aged just 15, he achieved it, quitting school and enlisting in the Royal Navy. Posted to Portsmouth Naval base, he was assigned to HMS Eagle, where he was unpopular with his shipmates. They found him to be cocky and arrogant and also prone to aggressive behavior when he'd been drinking. Drinking, in fact, had become David McGreavy's chief form of recreation. And it often got him into trouble. On one occasion, he broke into an officer's quarters and started a fire in a waste bin. He'd later claim that the fire started accidentally after he dropped his cigarette but the stunt nonetheless earned him 90 days in the brig.

In January 1971, McGreavy was transferred from HMS Eagle to a shore-based job at the Portsmouth dockyard. Not long after, he began corresponding with a young woman named Mary. After a series of letters, he finally got to meet Mary and was instantly smitten. Just a week later, he proposed and she accepted. Not everyone was thrilled by the engagement though. Mary had a serious spinal problem which might one day leave her completely paralyzed. David's mother wondered how her impulsive and somewhat irresponsible son would be able to handle such a situation but David was not to be deflected. He was marrying Mary, and that was that.

But then, in August 1981, came a development that might well have derailed his marriage plans. He was drummed out of the navy after yet another breach of discipline. He returned to his parents' home in the city of Worcester, in the English midlands. Disillusioned and despondent, he began drinking heavily, flitting from one job to another, verbally abusing his parents even while he was living under their roof and contributing nothing to the household. His only source of solace seemed to be his fiancée who he planned on marrying early in the new year. Mary had told him that she'd be quite happy with a small civil ceremony but David would hear nothing of that. He wanted a big church wedding followed by a lavish reception. How he planned on paying for all this is anyone's guess. That, in any case, was a question that would never need to be answered. Mary called off the engagement on New Year's Eve, 1971, leaving David devastated.

During the early months of 1972, McGreavy descended ever deeper into the bottle. He refused to work or even to look for a job, instead hanging around his parents' home in a blur of alcohol-fueled indignation. Eventually, they'd had enough and asked him to move out. Casting around for a place to stay, he convinced an old school friend, Clive Ralph, to let him crash at his place in the Rainbow Hill area of Worcester.

Conditions in the Ralph household were hardly ideal. Clive and his young wife Elsie already had two children, three-year-old Paul and 20-month-old Dawn and Elsie was pregnant with their third. The house that they rented on Gillam Street had only two bedrooms and so McGreavy shared with Paul while Dawn slept in her parents' bedroom. When the new baby, Samantha, arrived in September 1972, there were six people living in the tiny residence.

But, at least, McGreavy's presence offered some benefit to the cash-strapped couple. He'd since found work at a factory and paid £6 per week board and lodging. He even occasionally helped with the cooking and he was good with the children. That proved to be a boon when Samantha was old enough for Elsie to go back to work at the Punchbowl Tavern in nearby Ronkswood. With both parents working long hours, McGreavy often filled the role of babysitter. The Ralphs trusted him implicitly, even if he could be a bit obnoxious when he'd been drinking. No one had any inkling that he might hurt a child. No one, that is, until the night of Friday, April 13, 1973.

The evening had started in typical fashion for McGreavy. He'd finished his shift and had then gone to a local pub with a workmate. There, they'd played a few games of darts while each downed six or seven pints of beer. However, as so often happened when McGreavy was drinking, the bonding session came to a bad end. A tussle ensued after he dropped a cigarette into his friend's drink. It might well have ended in a full-blown fight if Clive Ralph hadn't arrived at that moment to take McGreavy home.

Elsie had a shift at the Punchbowl that night and McGreavy had promised to look after the children when Clive went to pick her up. Usually, Clive would leave about a half-hour early so he could enjoy a pint while he waited for last round to be called. And so it was this night. Clive Ralph drove away from his home at around 10:15 p.m., leaving his kids tucked up in bed and David McGreavy dozing in an armchair. He had no idea that he would never see his children alive again.

We do not know exactly what happened inside the Ralph
residence that night. All we know is what the police were able to
surmise from the evidence in the bloody aftermath. Sometime
between 10:15 and 11:15, nine-month-old Samantha started
crying, waking McGreavy from his drunken half-sleep. McGreavy
would have likely dealt with this situation many times in the past
but on this occasion, his temper got the better of him. Unable to
quiet the toddler down, he strangled her. Then he started beating
her, inflicting a compound fracture to her fragile skull. His
bloodlust still unsated, he fetched a razor from the bathroom and
started cutting the baby's tiny corpse, inflicting horrendous
injuries.

Next, McGreavy turned his attention to the older children. Dawn,
who he'd so often bounced upon his knee, was strangled to death
before her throat was sliced upon with a razor. Paul too, was
strangled before McGreavy got to work with the blade. Still
dissatisfied with his handiwork, the killer then fetched a pickaxe
handle from the basement and began pounding the lifeless bodies
to a pulp. He then carried the tiny corpses outside and impaled
them on the railings fronting the house.

It is impossible for any normal person to understand the
psychology of a person who could commit such an atrocity. Not
only had McGreavy ended the lives of three innocent young babes,
but here he was displaying his bloody handiwork for the world to
see. And if there was one mercy to this terrible saga it is that
someone did see and that someone called the police. By the time
Clive and Elsie arrived home, the police had cordoned off the area,
thus sparing them from the sight of their butchered children.

It did not take the police long to figure out who the perpetrator was. The children had been left in the care of David McGreavy and now McGreavy was missing. A search was launched and found him just hours later, aimlessly wandering the streets. "What's this about?" he said as he was placed under arrest.

At first, McGreavy denied any involvement in the children's deaths. Then he offered an enigmatic explanation. "It was me," he said, "but it wasn't me." He then went on to describe, in graphic detail, what he'd done to the children. More than one experienced detective had to leave the room as McGreavy nonchalantly retold the horrific events of that night. He was then formally charged with three counts of murder.

David McGreavy appeared at the Worcester Magistrates court on Thursday, June 28 1973, nine weeks after the killings. He made no pretense at innocence, entering a guilty plea and accepting the sentence of twenty years to life. It was less than the parents of the murdered children had expected. Still, few expected that McGreavy would ever be released. It was fully expected that he would die behind bars.

Like most child killers, David McGreavy's life in prison has not been easy. He has been harassed by fellow prisoners and at times violently assaulted. His cell has been trashed and his belongings urinated and defecated upon. He has spent long months in isolation for his own protection. And he continues to be a figure who stirs controversy.

In 2006, while preparing for a parole hearing, McGreavy was allowed to stay at a bail hostel in Liverpool and was even permitted to walk the streets without supervision. However, a journalist from a local newspaper had been tipped off and after a picture of the notorious child killer appeared in the press there was a public outcry. McGreavy was returned to prison where he remains to this day. He has thus far served over forty years, twice his minimum sentence. Yet there are those who believe that he has not yet repaid his debt to society. Many believe that he never will.

Death for Hire

The suburb of Rivercrest, on the western edge of Fort Worth, Texas is an area of stately mansions, many of them occupied by the city's wealthiest and most affluent families. It is hardly the sort of place where you would expect a bloody murder to occur but that is exactly what happened in the early morning hours of Thursday, March 12, 1992. At around 3:40 a.m. on that morning a Rivercrest resident was awakened by persistent banging on his front door. Going to answer it, he was shocked to find his neighbor, Jack Koslow, dressed only in his boxer shorts and covered in blood. Koslow appeared dazed and was quite obviously injured. "Call 911," he gasped. "For God's sake, please call 911."

Police and paramedics were quickly on the scene and immediately entered the Koslow residence. Following Koslow's direction, they went directly to the master bedroom on the upper floor. There, they found 40-year-old Caren Koslow, or at least what remained of her. The woman had suffered a savage beating, one of the worst that any of the officers could ever recall seeing. In addition, her throat had been slashed, the cuts running so deep that she had almost been decapitated. The weapon that had potentially inflicted the cuts lay on the floor nearby. So too did a shotgun, although it was empty and had not recently been fired. The bed, carpet, walls and even the ceiling were liberally spattered with blood. It was a savage, savage murder and the police thought they already had a very good idea as to who had committed it.

In any case of spousal homicide, the surviving partner is always the first suspect. There is a good reason for this. Experience has taught the police that most murder victims know their killer and that quite often that killer is their nearest and dearest. And so investigators started questioning Jack Koslow and the answers he gave did nothing to discourage their initial impression that he had murdered his wife.

For starters, there were the injuries that Koslow had suffered. These were not trivial. He had been beaten and slashed and there were defensive wounds to his hands and arms, including what appeared to be bite marks. But how had he survived when his wife had been so savagely slain?

Koslow's account was garbled and often contradictory. He said that two men had come into his bedroom in the dead of night, kicking in the door to gain entry. They had ordered him and his wife to lie on the floor and begun beating them with iron bars. Koslow had managed to break free and run to a closet where he kept his shotgun. But the weapon was unloaded and as he tried to slot a shell into the chamber he was attacked again. He then managed to get to his bedside table where he kept a .32-caliber pistol in a drawer. Again a struggle ensued during which a shot was fired. The attackers then broke off and fled.

The story sounded farfetched to investigators and it contained inconsistencies. For one thing, Koslow insisted that he had armed the burglar alarm before retiring to bed. So why hadn't it sounded? The security company was able to clear up that little mystery. The alarm had indeed been armed. But it had later been deactivated. And who had the code? Koslow admitted that it was only him and his wife.

And then there was the 911 call. Why hadn't Koslow made it from his own home? Why had he run to a neighbor? Koslow couldn't say but the investigators had an idea. They believed he wanted to establish a time of death. And that time, according to the medical examiner, was inconsistent with the evidence. The M.E. thought that Caren Koslow may have died four hours before her husband called it in.

As for the motive for the attack, Koslow had no idea who might have wanted to harm him or his wife. The police had been wondering about that too. Koslow's wallet, containing about $120 had been taken. So too had an expensive wristwatch but other valuables had gone untouched. In any case, this did not look like any burglary-gone-wrong that the investigators had ever seen. This was way too violent. This was personal.

To the detectives leading the investigation, to the press and to the general population, Jack Koslow had already been tried in the court of public opinion and found guilty. The motive? Well, there was evidence that the couple had been seeing a marriage counsellor. And there was always money. Jack Koslow, an ex-military helicopter pilot, was not well off but his wife was from a wealthy Texas oil family. Also Jack had recently been laid off from his job.

And so, as a bruised and battered Jack Koslow attended his wife's funeral, the police firmly believed that they had already solved their case. They had a wealth of circumstantial evidence. All they needed was a few forensics to back them up and they'd have their man. Most promising of all were the bite marks to Koslow's hand. If they could prove through forensic odontology that Caren Koslow's teeth had made those marks, they'd have a slam dunk. While they waited on those results they publicly denied Jack Koslow was a suspect. In private, though...

But then, two weeks into the investigation, the police got a surprise tip-off, one that would veer the case in an entirely different direction. The caller was a frightened young man who said that he had some information on the Koslow case and that he had "some things you need to take a look at." Those items turned out to be a bloody pry bar and some extremely blood-spattered clothing. The informant said a friend had given him the items the day after Caren Koslow was killed. The friend had asked him to get rid of the items, explaining that they had been used in a murder. But then the informant had seen the story of the murder on the news and had decided he didn't want to be involved in disposing of evidence. He'd been holding onto the objects ever since, agonizing over what he should do with them.

The informant's friend turned out to be a 19-year-old man named Jeffrey Dillingham. And as detectives started looking into his background they began wondering if they had the right man. Dillingham made a most unlikely killer. He had no police record and was a former honor student who now managed the graveyard shift at an Arlington video store. He was from a stable upper-middleclass background and had a fiancée who he planned on marrying in the summer. When the police carried out a raid on his place of work on March 24, he surrendered without a fight. Back at the station, he almost immediately started talking.

Dillingham said that he and a friend, 19-year-old Brian Salter, had entered the Koslow residence on the night of the murder, made their way to the couple's bedroom and attacked them. He had been carrying an iron pry bar while Salter had been armed with a hunting knife. Describing the attack, he said: "I hit Mr. Koslow in the back of the head, on the neck. Then I hit Mrs. Koslow, and I hit Mr. Koslow some more. She was screaming and I hit her with the pry bar and she continued to scream and I hit her in the throat and then she laid down and Brian cut her throat." She then described struggling with Jack Koslow, the gun going off and how that caused him and Salter to flee for fear that it would alert the neighbors.

But what the investigators still did not understand was why? Did Dillingham know the Koslows? "Not them," he said, "but I know their daughter, Kristi. She's the one who hired me and Brian. She promised me a million dollars out of her inheritance." Noticing the look of disbelief that passed between his interrogators, Dillingham added: "Who do you think it was that gave us the alarm code and a map of the house?"

Brian Salter and Kristi Koslow, Jack's 17-year-old daughter from a previous marriage, were taken into custody that same day. Like Dillingham, they made no pretense at innocence and seemed almost eager to admit their involvement. Kristi said that she had planned the murder because she didn't get along with her father after he'd married Caren. That, however, may have been subsidiary to her real motive. She stood to inherit $12 million from the deaths of her father and stepmother.

Dillingham, Salter and Koslow were tried separately for the murder of Caren Koslow. In the run up to the trial, all three of the accused were offered plea deals which Salter and Koslow accepted but which Dillingham refused. Salter and Koslow were each given life sentences with parole eligibility but for Dillingham it was death, a sentence that would eventually be carried out by lethal injection on November 1, 2000.

Jeffrey Dillingham was 27 years old on the day that he was put to death at the Huntsville Unit in Huntsville, Texas. He appeared calm as he entered the death chamber. "I would just like to apologize to the victims of the family for what I did," he said in his final statement. "I take full responsibility for that poor woman's death and for the pain and suffering I inflicted on Mr. Koslow." Looking towards his family, he then mouthed, "I love you all, you all take care." Then he smiled and winked before letting out a gasp as the drugs took effect. He died at 6:28 p.m., eight minutes after the lethal dose was administered.

The Hit

On the morning of June 16, 2001, 44-year-old Jeff Zack got into his Ford SUV and drove away from his home in Akron, Ohio. Zack's intended destination was a catering warehouse where he planned on buying supplies to restock the vending machines he operated. This was part of his usual Saturday routine, a tedious job but one that had to be done. Empty machines put no money into his bank account.

Zack was somewhat distracted on this particular morning. A romantic entanglement had recently ended and he was trying to think of a way that he might convince his errant lover to return. As such, he did not notice the black motorcycle that drifted away from the curb at the end of his street and fell in behind him. He also didn't notice the precarious angle of his fuel gauge until the warning light popped on and roused him from his funk. Then he cast his eye along the road ahead and spotted a gas station. Engaging his turn signal, he eased towards the side of the road and mounted the incline towards the pumps. Behind him, the black-clad motorcyclist made the same turn.

This particular gas station was full service and so Zack waited in his car for an attendant to reach him. While he sat there, still not paying particular attention to his surroundings, the motorcyclist came to a stop behind him. He was dressed all in black leather and wearing a black helmet with a tinted visor that hid his features. Unzipping his jacket, he reached his hand inside and it came back holding a gun. Then he walked calmly around the SUV to the passenger side window, lifted the weapon and fired a single shot that shattered the glass and hit Jeff Zack squarely in the head. Zack was dead by the time he slumped forward onto the steering wheel and ejected a spray of blood onto the inside of the windshield.

Carolyn Hyson, a pump attendant at the station, was walking towards the SUV when she heard the sharp snap of the pistol. Recognizing it as a gunshot, she froze on the spot, too afraid to take another step. That was when she saw a man emerge from behind the Ford. He looked directly at her, she'd later tell the police, but she couldn't see his face because the visor of his helmet was blacked out. For a moment that seemed like an eternity, he just stood there, holding the gun by his side, looking at her. She felt certain that she was about to he shot as well but then the man reached into his jacket and holstered his weapon. Then he walked casually to his motorcycle, mounted it and roared off into the distance. Badly shaken, Carolyn fumbled for her phone and dialed 911.

Police and an ambulance were soon on the scene, even if the latter was superfluous. Jeff Zack was dead, killed by a single, large-caliber bullet to the head. The shooter, meanwhile, was long gone and although Carolyn provided a good description of motorcycle – a black-and-gray racing-style Honda with lime-green stripes –the police roadblocks that were hastily set up to apprehend him came up empty. Unbeknownst to the police, he'd already crossed the state line into Pennsylvania.

From the outset, this was a frustrating case for investigators, beginning with the surfeit of individuals who might have wanted Jeff Zack dead. Zack, they learned, was not a popular man. A former Israeli paratrooper, he was known as a difficult, argumentative type with a short fuse. He had also been involved in several shady business deals, one of which had led to federal charges in Arizona and had ended up costing him his stockbroking business. Thereafter, he'd moved his family to the city of Stow, Ohio, an affluent enclave within the metropolitan bounds of Akron. There, he was soon involved in a series of petty disputes with his neighbors.

Detectives learned other details about their victim, too, details that might well have provided motive for murder. Zack was a brazen womanizer, who had arrests on record in Arizona for operating an escort service and for attempting to molest an adolescent girl. Perhaps more pertinently, he'd been involved in an ongoing affair with a woman named Cynthia George, wife of a wealthy Akron businessman. According to Zack's wife, Bonnie, Zack had ended the relationship after she'd found out about it and confronted him. But Zack's cellphone records told a different story. He was still in touch with George, sometimes staying on the line with her for

hours. Might this relationship have been the motive for murder?
Might Cynthia George's jealous husband have decided to end his
wife's dalliance with a bullet?

That theory was instantly shot down when the police interviewed
Ed George. Older than his wife by fifteen years, George did not fit
the physical type of the shooter, did not own a motorcycle and, in
any case, had a cast-iron alibi. The possibility still existed, of
course, that he had hired someone to do the deed for him. But the
police soon abandoned that possibility for a more promising line
of inquiry. It appeared that Jeff Zack had not been the only one
enjoying the company of the voluptuous Mrs. George. Cynthia had
recently taken up with a new lover, a burly, 36-year-old trucker
named John Zaffino.

Zaffino was quickly tracked down and while he admitted to being
Cynthia George's lover, he denied killing his rival for her affections.
Cynthia had, in any case, ended things with Zack, he said. Also, he
could not have killed Zack as he was at a car show in Pennsylvania
at the time of the shooting. An alibi witness verified this. As for
Cynthia George, she was saying nothing, with her husband's
expensive lawyers thwarting all attempts by detectives to
interview her.

And so the case stalled and would continue to stall over the next
year. Then, in 2002, the offer of a reward finally coaxed an
important piece of information out of a potential witness. The
tipster was Christine Todaro, Zaffino's former wife, who said that
Zaffino had made a "kind of confession" to her at around the time
of the murder. He had told her that he had beaten up on a "white-

haired Israeli." When she'd pressed him for details, he'd told her: "Let's just say the guy's going to have a hard time parting his hair from now on."

This was interesting information. Not only had Zaffino accurately described the victim, but the statement had been made within days of Zack's death. Investigators were not naive enough, however, to think that it would stand up in a court of law. They needed more and they soon had it. Ongoing efforts to trace the shooter's motorcycle eventually paid off when it was tracked to a bike shop in Murray, Pennsylvania. Incidentally, the shop was owned by the fiancée of John Zaffino's ex-wife. Questioned about it, the man said that Zaffino had given the bike to them in lieu of arrear alimony payments. Following the paper trail, detectives learned that Zaffino had purchased the gray-and-black Honda CBR 1000 under the name "John Smith" on May 24, three weeks before the murder. He'd handed it over to his wife the day after Jeff Zack was shot.

The evidence was stacking up. But detectives were acutely aware that their case was circumstantial. There were plenty of gray-and-black Hondas on the road. What they needed was an admission from Zaffino. In order to get it, they convinced Christine Todaro to wear a wire and also to record phone calls between her and Zaffino. The suspect, however, was growing increasingly paranoid. During one conversation, he asked Christine outright if she was recording him. On another occasion, he threatened her not to cooperate with the police. And over the three months of the operation, he never once said anything incriminating.

Other avenues, however, were proving far more productive. Zaffino's alibi was shot down when police checked his cellphone records and proved that he had not been in Pennsylvania as he'd claimed. In fact, he'd made a call to a friend just minutes after the shooting and that call was made from an area close to the crime scene. He had only arrived at the Pennsylvania car show two hours later.

At the end of September, John Zaffino was arrested and charged with aggravated murder. The police were confident that he was the black-clad man on the motorcycle, and they soon learned that the gas station shooting had not been the first attempt on Jeff Zack's life. Just weeks before the murder, Zaffino had been questioned by a police officer as he sat in his car at Cuyahoga Valley National Park. He had been found to be in possession of an empty holster. When asked about it, he'd said that he had forgotten his gun at home. A few days later, a visitor had found a .32-caliber pistol discarded in the park, close to the spot where Zaffino had been questioned. Zaffino had purchased a .32-caliber just a few days before but couldn't produce it when asked. Police surmised that he'd come to the park that day to shoot Zack (who was also visiting the area) but had thrown the weapon away when the police officer had approached him. Days later, Zaffino had purchased a .357 Magnum, the type of weapon that had ultimately ended Jeff Zack's life.

John Zaffino went to trial on February 26, 2003 and was found guilty of first degree murder and sentenced to life in prison with no parole for at least 23 years. However, the D.A. considered this a job only half done. He firmly believed that Cynthia George had been involved in the conspiracy to kill Jeff Zack. Proving it, though, would be a different matter.

John Zaffino was certainly no help. He remained steadfastly loyal to his former lover and refused to say anything. But that is not to say that the police were without evidence. There were the phone calls that had passed between George and Zaffino in the proximity to the murder. And there was an unexplained $5,300 withdrawal from her bank account, exactly the amount that Zaffino had paid for the Honda and a couple of helmets. There was also a two-hour call between George and Zack on the day Zaffino had been questioned in Cuyahoga Valley National Park. Investigators believed that the intention of that call had been to distract Zack, allowing Zaffino to creep up on him. As to motive, Zack was obsessed with George and continued to stalk her long after she'd told him that their relationship was over. People have been killed for less.

Cynthia George was arrested on January 10, 2005. Charged with complicity and conspiracy to commit aggravated murder, she appeared before the Akron Courts in November 2005. Her attorney had opted for a bench trial fearing that a jury might react emotionally to the evidence, rather than seeing it for what it was, a mish-mash of conjecture and supposition. But the move backfired. Judge Cosgrove weighed the evidence and found that there was sufficient cause to convict. The sentence was the same as that given to George's lover, John Zaffino – 23 years to life.

Cynthia George, however, would serve just over a year of that sentence. In March 2007, the Ninth Ohio District Court of Appeals overturned Judge Cosgrove's decision, citing insufficient evidence to convict. Cynthia George was declared not guilty and therefore immune from any future legal action under the double jeopardy rule. Given the evidence presented at trial, it was probably the right decision. We shall never know for sure if she really was innocent of involvement in Jeff Zack's death.

Death Metal

Fabio Tollis was just a kid, a sixteen-year-old who loved heavy metal music and was blessed with a voice that had gained him an audition with a local death metal band known as the Beasts of Satan. Fabio had shone at that audition and had been welcomed into the fold by band members Andrea Volpe, Nicola Sapone and Andrea Bontade. Thereafter, they'd done a few gigs together and Fabio had loved every minute of it. He was living the dream. If the other members' views on subjects like Satanism were somewhat extreme, he was happy to go along with them. After all, Satanism and the occult were core lyrical themes in their music. To him, it was all part of the image.

On the evening of Saturday, January 17, 1998, Fabio was drinking at a heavy metal bar known as the Midnight Pub, when his bandmates showed up. They said that they were going into the woods to do some drugs and participate in a Satanic ritual and invited him to join them. Fabio was at first uncertain. But his girlfriend, 19-year-old Chiara Marino, was heavily into Satanism

and told him that it would be "fun." The group then set off for the
Somma Lombardo woods, northeast of Milan, Italy. Their usual
entourage of hangers-on – Pietro Guerrieri, Mario Maccione, Paolo
Leoni, Marco Zampollo, and Eros Monterosso – accompanied them.
Drummer Andrea Bontade, however, opted out, saying he had a
headache and was going home. Most likely, he knew what was
coming.

There was a full moon out that night and the eerie shadows it cast
off the skeletal trees were befitting of the ritual that was about to
unfold. The group lit candles and arranged them in a circle on the
leaf-strewn floor; they cranked up the music on the boom-box
they'd brought with them; lines of cocaine were snorted and a
heroin pipe was passed around, along with bottles of beer. It was
all fun and games until things suddenly turned ugly.

No one would later say exactly how it had started but it appears
that Andrea Volpe had begun acting aggressively towards Chiara
Marino, the only female in the group. He accused her of being an
enemy of Satan and the "personification of the Virgin Mary." Then
he came at her, holding a knife. Fabio Tollis, seeing that his
girlfriend was in danger, jumped to his feet and tried to tackle
Volpe. But he was struck from behind by a hammer wielded by one
of the group. Then, as he collapsed to the forest floor, the others
joined the fray, kicking, punching, slashing with knives, swinging
with the hammer in a frenzied attack.

Fabio and Chiara never stood a chance. Within minutes, they were
overcome, their bodies lying broken and bleeding on the forest
floor. Then, the killers dug a hole and dragged the corpses in,

urinating on them before covering them with dirt. "Now you're both zombies!" one of them screamed, "Try to get out of this hole, if you dare!"

The following day, Michele Tollis, Fabio's father, went to his local police station and reported his son missing. According to Michele, Fabio had gone to a gig at the Midnight Pub the previous evening and had never come home.

"You're sure he's not with friends?" the police sergeant wanted to know.

"Certain," Michele responded sliding a picture of Fabio over the desk. Then, seeing the sergeant's response to the picture of the burly, long-haired teen, he interjected. "He's not that kind of boy."

"Very well," the officer said with a sigh. "We'll see what we can do."

But, in truth, the police did very little about finding Fabio Tollis, especially after they learned that his girlfriend was also missing. The obvious conclusion was that the teenagers had run away together and that was borne out by Fabio's bandmates. "I had a feeling they might hit the road," Andrea Volpe told the police. "Fabio spoke about it all the time," Nicola Sapone confirmed.

And so, the police marked Fabio and Chiara as runaways and stopped looking for them. Michele, however, was not prepared to accept that his son would have run off without a word. The two had a close relationship, a good relationship. Michele had never encroached on his son's freedom. He'd always encouraged his music career. Fabio had no reason to run away.

Over the next six years, Michele Tollis continued hunting for his son, visiting heavy metal bars and attending concerts and festivals across Europe. At each of these events he handed out leaflets and made inquiries. He also interrogated Fabio's friends, questioning them so frequently that his attempts at playing amateur detective became somewhat of a standing joke.

Yet Tollis's investigative instincts were to prove remarkably accurate. He quickly began to suspect that his son's former bandmates, Volpe and Sapone, were hiding something. Six months after Fabio's disappearance, the band's drummer, Andrea Bontade had committed suicide and the Beasts of Satan had split up. Tollis, however, had continued to monitor the surviving band members, keeping a detailed dossier on each of them. Eventually, his efforts paid off.

On January 24, 2004, Michele Tollis was watching a local news program when he saw a report on a particularly brutal murder that had been committed in the nearby town of Golasecca. The victim was a young woman named Mariangela Pezzotta, who had been shot and then buried alive in a greenhouse. But what really caught Tollis's attention was the name of the main suspect – Andrea Volpe.

Volpe had initially denied even knowing Mariangela Pezzotta. But he'd eventually cracked and admitted that she was his ex-girlfriend and that he'd invited her to dinner with the express intention of killing her. According to Volpe, he'd planned on shooting Pezzotta. However, when he'd drawn his gun, Pezzotta had made a grab for it. A struggle had then ensued during which the weapon had discharged, hitting Pezzotta and severely injuring her. Volpe had then panicked and called Nicola Sapone, asking for his help.

Sapone had been furious when he'd found that Pezzotta was still alive. "You can't even kill a person!" he'd screamed. Yet he, too, couldn't bring himself to finish off the mortally wounded woman. Instead, they'd driven her to the home of Volpe's girlfriend, 18-year-old Elisabetta Ballarin. There, they'd buried Pezzotta in a shallow grave in the greenhouse, covering her with earth while she was still alive.

Might they have gotten away with this ill-conceived murder? Possibly. But Volpe and Ballarin then put themselves in the frame by getting high and driving Pezzotta's vehicle to a nearby lake, where they planned on submerging it. Instead they slammed into a crash barrier, leading to their arrest for driving under the influence. It was after the police traced the vehicle and started asking questions about its owner that Volpe broke down and admitted murder.

But now the police had another situation to deal with. Michele
Tollis had arrived at the precinct with his thick dossier on Volpe
and was insisting that detectives question Volpe about his son's
disappearance. When they eventually did, they were in for a
surprise. Not only did Volpe admit to the murders of Chiara
Marino and Fabio Tollis but he explained how they were linked to
the Pezzotta case. "Maria knew too much," he said. "She knew
about the murders of Fabio and Chiara. I was afraid she'd talk to
someone about them." Later, as part of a plea deal, Volpe would
lead the police to the bodies, buried for six years in the Somma
Lombardo woods.

Andrea Volpe went on trial in February 2005 and was sentenced
to 30 years in prison. Four months later in June 2005, it was the
turn of Nicola Sapone, the group leader and supposed mastermind
behind the killings. He received a life sentence. Pietro Guerrieri,
Paolo Leoni, Marco Zampollo, and Eros Monterosso all got long
prison terms while Mario Maccione, who was considered to have
played a minor role, was cleared. Elisabetta Ballarin got 23 years
for her part in the killing of Mariangela Pezzotta.

The Beasts of Satan were behind bars but still the police were left
to wonder if they had uncovered the full extent of the group's
activities. Certainly, they had been involved in the suicide of
Andrea Bontade. Mario Maccione had confirmed as much. After the
drummer refused to participate in the murders of Marino and
Tollis, the other band members had turned on him, harassing him
to the point where he'd eventually taken his own life. The group is
also suspected in a number of other unsolved murders in the area,
all of them with Satanic overtones.

Kill Him by Christmas

Sueanne Hobson

The problem with marrying for the second time, and marrying a widower who has a kid from his first marriage, is that you can never know how well you'll get on with your stepchild. Sueanne Hobson had found this out to her cost. When the divorced mother of two tied the knot with Ed Hobson in December 1978, she knew that his son Christen was a difficult boy. The 13-year-old attended a remedial school due, in part, to his frequent temper tantrums and aggression towards other children. And he was no different at home. Chris hated his new stepmother and his 13-year-old stepsister, Suzanne, and he wasn't afraid to show it. The fights at the family's home in Overland Park, Kansas were frequent and ferocious. Ed Hobson found himself constantly having to play the role of arbitrator.

Add to this volatile mix, Sueanne's 17-year-old son from her previous marriage and you had a toxic mix just waiting for a spark to ignite it. Jimmy Crumm, like Chris, was a problem child although for different reasons. He was a junkie and ne'er-do-good who had started drinking alcohol at the age of ten and had graduated from there to popping copious amounts of Valium and other prescription drugs. He was also a petty criminal who had been in and out of trouble with the law, mostly for theft and burglary. He had a habit to feed after all, and it wasn't as though he was going to get a job.

It goes without saying that Chris and Jimmy didn't see eye to eye. Jimmy didn't like the way that Chris spoke to his mother and sister. Chris didn't like Jimmy lazing around the house sponging off his father. In a war that was already blowing hot, a new battle line was drawn. And on April 17, 1980, it claimed its first casualty

April 17th was the day that Ed Hobson called the police and reported his 13-year-old son missing. A cruiser was then dispatched to the Hobson residence where an apparently distraught Ed and Sueanne answered questions. Ed tearfully admitted that Chris "had his problems" but insisted that he was "a good boy." He emphatically denied suggestions that the boy might have run away, even after Chris's billfold was found at the Metcalf South Shopping Center on the other side of town. A search was launched for the boy but it was abandoned after a few days when no trace of him was found. Ed Hobson, who'd lost his first wife to cancer and his daughter to suicide, was left with another loss to grieve.

Just over two weeks later, on May 3, 1980, two boys went fishing at a creek near Hillsdale Lake in rural Miami County. Part of the ritual, of course, involved digging up some worms for bait and the boys soon found a likely spot and began scraping at the loose soil.

They were just a few inches down when they were suddenly hit by a horrendous stench. Then one of them spotted something in the dirt and in the next moment they were staggering back and then running, leaving their fishing poles behind them.

Police officers and a crime scene unit were soon at the location and an evacuation of the gravesite delivered up the badly decomposed body of a young boy. It was immediately evident that he'd been shot, the weapon most likely a shotgun. It did not take long for the police to make an identification. Christen Hobson had been found.

From the very start, investigators believed that someone in the extended Hobson family was responsible. And those suspicions quickly zeroed in on Jimmy Crumm. Brought in for questioning, the young man was quite obviously nervous, fidgeting in his chair and refusing to make eye contact. It didn't take long before he broke down and confessed, also implicating a friend of his, 16-year-old Paul Sorrentino.

According to Crumm, he and Sorrentino had picked up Chris at the Hobson home on April 17, forced him into their car and then driven him around for a while before eventually stopping on a quiet country road next to a creek. There they'd ordered the terrified boy from the car, thrown him a shovel and ordered him to start digging. While a sobbing Chris was evacuating his own grave, Crumm and Sorrentino stood doing some drugs, laughing and taunting their victim. Then they made him lie down in the hole to "try it for size." Deciding that it was deep enough, they forced him to kneel. The killers then counted to three before opening fire with their shotguns, hitting Chris in the neck and chest. As the boy lay dying in his makeshift grave, Sorrentino stood over him and fired twice more, ending his life.

It was a harrowing tale but one that had not yet delivered its most shocking detail. Asked why he had killed Chris, Crumm said that he had no malice towards his stepbrother. It had been a business transaction, pure and simple. The murder had been carried out at the behest of his mother.

While officers digested this unexpected confession, Crumm continued to elaborate. His mother hated Chris, he said, and complained that he was destroying her marriage. She had been planning to get rid of him for over a year. First, she'd tried to kill him herself, doping his ice cream with ground up Quaaludes in an effort to cause an overdose. When that had failed, she'd turned to Jimmy alternately cajoling and pleading with him. After all she'd done for him, she said, he should be willing to do this "one small thing" for her. When her pleas had fallen on deaf ears, she'd resorted to bribery. She'd promised to buy Jimmy a car and to give Sorrentino $350 to pay for repairs to his motorcycle. Crumm and Sorrentino then agreed to carry out the murder. Sueanne had urged them to get it done before Christmas so that she "wouldn't have to buy a present for the little shit."

Sueanne Hobson was furious when confronted with her son's allegations. She emphatically denied having anything to do with the murder and said that Jimmy was trying to get back at her because she had recently ejected him from her home after she'd caught him stealing from her. She did, however, confess to one thing. She admitted to being aware of the murder. According to her version of events, Jimmy had confessed the killing to her days after it happened. He said that Paul Sorrentino had done the actual shooting but that he had been present and was therefore equally culpable. He had warned her not to say anything or Sorrentino would "kill them all."

Out of fear and out of love for her son Sueanne had decided not to report the crime. She had even driven out to the Metcalf South Shopping Center and left Chris's wallet there so that it would appear that he'd run away. She admitted that she'd had problems with Chris but denied any involvement in his death.

The police were now left with a problem. Who was telling the truth and who was lying? On the face of it, Sueanne Hobson was the more reliable witness. Her son, after all, was a junkie and petty thief. She was an apparently upstanding citizen, with no criminal record. What was needed was an independent witness to break the impasse. They found one in thirteen-year-old, Suzanne Hobson. And it wasn't good news for Sueanne.

According to Suzanne she had heard Jimmy and Sueanne plotting to murder Chris and had heard Jimmy tell her that he had found someone to help him. On the day of the murder, she had heard her mother tell Jimmy that she would get Ed out of the house so that he and his accomplice could kidnap Chris. A few days later, her mother had told her that Jimmy had "taken care of their problem."

Faced with these new allegations, Sueanne admitted that she had spoken to Jimmy about Chris. But she said that she had only asked him to speak to the boy about his behavior. That is most probably the conversation that Suzanne had overheard. If so, she had misinterpreted it. Unfortunately for Sueanne, the D.A. thought differently, she was arrested and charged with murder.

The trial of Sueanne Hobson was the most high-profile ever held in Johnson County, with crowds queuing by 7 a.m. every morning in the hope of gaining a seat in the courthouse. On the stand, Sueanne cut a less than sympathetic figure with her "icy glares" and her defiant, sometimes sarcastic answers. At times she struggled to keep her voice under control, at others she dabbed at her eyes ("pretending to cry" according to at least one newspaper).

But all of those histrionics were to no avail. Once Sueanne's daughter took the stand she was effectively doomed. Despite protesting her innocence, she was convicted of first-degree murder and conspiracy to commit murder. She was sentenced to life in prison and would spend 31 years behind bars before gaining parole at the ninth attempt. As for her co-accused, Jimmy Crumm was convicted of first-degree murder, while Paul Sorrentino was convicted as an accomplice. Both received life sentences. Crumm was paroled in January 1999, Sorrentino in April 2000.

There is one further twist to the story. After Sueanne's conviction, Ed Hobson divorced her although they re-married a few years later while she was serving her sentence. He would become a tireless campaigner for her release. At the same time, he was also an active and prominent member of the support group, *Parents of*

Murdered Children. Needless to say, this duality caused some consternation.

Desperate Measures

George Maben

Carshalton Beeches is an affluent suburb to the south of greater London in the so-called stockbroker-belt. It is a peaceful enclave of leafy streets and tranquil parks with natural springs and ponds adding to its aesthetic appeal. It even has a waterfall, situated in the green expanse of Grove Park. The hustle and bustle of the capital city, just ten miles away, might as well be another world. Property does not come cheap in Carshalton and the suburb's residents reflect that. They are, in the main, city professionals and wealthy retirees. Needless to say, crime in the area is virtually non-existent.

Maureen Cosgrove had called Carshalton home for many years. The 65-year-old retired teacher was still active in the community and volunteered regularly at Seaton House, a girls' preparatory school. She was also involved in local charities, including Radio Lollipop, a program devoted to providing care and entertainment to sick children. Aside from that, Maureen was devoted to her four children and seven grandchildren. She was well-liked by neighbors who described her as a "sweet, lovely person."

Maureen's life, however, was not without its problems. In 2007, her husband Terence, a financial consultant, had been found hanging by his neck in a neighborhood park. Nobody knew why the well-liked Mr. Cosgrove would have decided to take his own life, although neighbors of the Cosgroves were quick to offer an opinion. They said it was all down to the couple's daughter, Lucy Rees.

It is said that there is a black sheep in every family and in the Cosgrove family that role was filled by 34-year-old Lucy. A single mother of two small children, Lucy had struggled throughout her adult life with drug addiction. It had cost her marriage and livelihood and almost seen her children taken away from her. But for the intervention of her parents, offering her and her brood a place to stay, that might well have happened. But Lucy's return to her parental home was not all sweetness and light. While Terrance and Maureen loved having their grandchildren around, relations with Lucy were sometimes strained. Arguments, at least according to neighbors, were frequent, and one of the biggest bones of contention was her choice in men. Maureen Cosgrove, in particular, did not like George Maben, her daughter's latest beau, a bone-idle Irishman who at 45 still lived with his mother. Even after her husband's death, Maureen continued to regard Maben with suspicion and disdain. It came as a shock therefore when Lucy announced that she was pregnant with Maben's child.

One can fully understand Maureen Cosgrove's despair at the situation. At 34, Lucy should have known better. She already had two children she was unable to support. To fall pregnant again, and by a man like George Maben, was reckless and foolhardy. Maben was hardly going to be able to provide for his child when he was unemployed and could barely look after himself. The burden, inevitably, was going to fall on Maureen's shoulders. It was a situation that drove an even larger wedge between Maureen and Maben. Before she had regarded him with a kind of polite disdain, now the disdain was of a less than civil variety.

On the morning of Tuesday, March 24, 2009, Maureen Cosgrove made her way to an appointment with her dentist, about a mile away from her home. Later that same morning, Lucy Rees and George Maben met up for a drink at a pub in Sutton, leaving a couple of hours later and going from there back to the house that Lucy shared with her mother. Maben, by his own admission, was dreading another visit with his girlfriend's mother. Encounters with Maureen had become more and more uncomfortable of late.

But George Maben would be spared coming face-to-face with his prospective mother-in-law on this particular day. On arriving at the house, he and Lucy saw immediately that something was wrong. The patio door stood open. Both of them knew that the fastidiously security-conscious Maureen always kept it closed. Then, as Lucy entered the kitchen, she let out a cry. Her mother lay on the ground, arms splayed to her sides, her eyes closed. Lucy rushed in, fell to her knees and tried to revive her mother. Getting no response, she ran to the phone and called for an ambulance.

The first responders were on the scene at around 2:20 p.m. but by then it was already clear to Lucy that her mother was beyond help. It was quite obvious that Maureen wasn't breathing. Tearfully, Lucy described to the paramedics how she'd arrived home to find her mother lying on the floor. How had this happened, she wanted to know. Had her mother suffered a stroke? A heart attack? She'd been in perfect health when she'd left the house earlier in the day. But although they weren't saying, the paramedics had already formed an opinion as to how Maureen had met her end. The telltale red welts on her neck were a dead giveaway. The first call they made was to the police.

Detective Chief Inspector (DCI) John McFarlane was among the first officers at the scene and it did not take him long to confirm the paramedics' findings. There was little doubt that this was a homicide but the thing that puzzled McFarlane was motive. His initial idea, that it might have been a burglary gone wrong, was quickly dismissed since the house had not been ransacked and nothing appeared to be missing. And the mystery was only deepened when officers started questioning the neighbors. No one had a single bad thing to say about Maureen Cosgrove, no one could think of anyone in the world who might have meant her harm.

The investigators' next step was to track the victim's movements in the hours leading up to her death. They learned that she had kept her dental appointment and had arrived home at around 11:20 a.m. Nothing unusual there. But then, the police got what appeared to be the first break in the case. A neighbor described a dark-colored Volvo station wagon that had been parked across the street when Mrs. Cosgrove arrived home, but was gone soon after.

Detectives immediately got to work trying to track down the driver. In the meantime, an autopsy had been conducted on Maureen Cosgrove's body and had determined that she'd died of asphyxia, caused by ligature strangulation.

As someone who had been present at the discovery of the body, George Maben was, of course, interviewed by police. He was frank in his description of his relationship with the victim, saying that it was "up and down," and offering that Maureen did not approve of him or of his two-year relationship with her daughter. Asked about his movements on the day of the murder, he said that he and Lucy had met at a pub in the nearby Sutton town center at 11:30 a.m., and had sat outside and had a drink. While they were there, Lucy had tried to phone her mother but had gotten no response. Lucy had then called her sister to see if she had seen or spoken to their mother, only to learn that she had not. After leaving the pub, he and Lucy had done some shopping before driving back to Maureen's house.

He then explained how they had found Maureen's body, adding that the back gate, laundry door and side door were all open when he and Lucy arrived which was unusual because Maureen was very security conscious. He then offered the opinion that Maureen had been killed during a burglary gone wrong and provided a piece of evidence the cops had not yet picked up on. Maureen's handbag was missing from the house, he said. Lucy had told him so.

There was one other thing to come out of this initial interview with Maben. One of the officers noticed an injury to one of his

hands, later described as a "friction mark." Asked how the injury
had occurred, Maben hesitated for just a moment before saying
that he'd got it scraping his hand against a wall while moving a
washing machine for his mother. The police had no reason to
disbelieve him.

The next phase of the investigation focused on tracking down Mrs.
Cosgrove's handbag. Lucy Rees confirmed to police that her
mother's bag was indeed missing and described it as navy blue,
with a long shoulder strap and a large flap over the front. A public
appeal was then issued, asking residents in the area to search their
gardens, in case the killer had discarded it as he made his getaway.
While that was underway, the police got a break in their other
search. The driver of the dark-colored Volvo was traced. However,
he was quickly eliminated from the investigation. Frustratingly, it
was back to square one.

As any homicide investigator will tell you, dead ends, false clues
and misleading information are all part of the job. Unlike in
Hollywood crime thrillers, clues are seldom obvious and they
hardly ever just fall together, as if by magic. Solving a murder is
meticulous, time-consuming work and quite often the most
mundane details might hold the key. With nowhere else to go,
detectives started going over what they had so far and soon picked
up on George Maben's hand injury. He'd said that he'd gotten it
moving a washing machine. Investigators decided to check if he
was telling the truth.

Within the next few days, officers called at the home in Rosehill,
where Maben lived with his mother. Mrs. Maben willingly allowed

them in and then led them to the appliance that Maben claimed to have moved. However, they found no indication that the washing machine had been moved recently. So had Maben lied about his hand injury and if so why? The police didn't want to jump to any conclusions just yet but they decided to focus the next phase of the investigation on Maben. From that point on, he became their main suspect.

And there was soon other evidence to back up their suspicions. While viewing CCTV footage from the pub where Maben had met Lucy on the day of the murder, they discovered that he'd arrived an hour later than he'd told them he had. Another lie. Then they carried out forensic tests on the red cardigan that Maureen Cosgrove had been wearing when she died and found a number of black fibers. Those fibers were matched to similar ones from the jacket Maben had worn that day. Finally, there was even more close circuit footage, this time from a bus stop near the Cosgrove home. Maben is seen alighting from a bus at around the time of the murder. He stops for a moment to pull on a pair of black gloves before walking on. The police were obviously keen to test those gloves but when they asked Maben to hand them over, he said that his dog had eaten them.

The police had now constructed a chilling picture of the murder of Maureen Cosgrove. They believed that Maben had gone to the Cosgrove residence on the morning of March 24, strangled Mrs. Cosgrove to death and then hurried to keep his date with Lucy. He'd then sat and calmly enjoyed a drink with his girlfriend knowing full-well that he'd just murdered her mother. His motive, according to police, was simple. He was tired of Maureen's negative attitude to him and afraid that she might eventually get through to Lucy and that Lucy would then dump him.

It was a convincing hypothesis and one that was supported by considerable evidence. But DCI McFarlane wanted more before moving in to arrest Maben. He therefore obtained authorization to place a bugging device inside Maben's car. It did not take long before Maben provided the evidence that the police needed. On Thursday, April 9, the listening device picked him up, apparently praying for forgiveness:

"Please God, help me. Help me and Lucy to be eliminated from all police inquiries and everything's all right. Please God, help me. God forgive me for what I have done. I just could not take it anymore. Every single day she was breaking me down. Please God, will you forgive me?"

It was as good a confession to murder. Maben was arrested the next day.

George Maben's trial took place at London's Old Bailey in November 2009. And with the excellent detective work done by the Metropolitan Police, there was never a chance that he would escape a conviction. However, Maben was fortunate to have his case heard before a judge who showed him far more compassion than Maben had shown his victim.

Judge Jeremy Roberts sentenced Maben to life in prison but set the parole period at just 13 years. In his summation, the judge noted that Maben had been driven to "desperate measures" for fear of losing the woman he loved. He also noted that Maben's prayer for forgiveness showed that he was remorseful. Ironically, Maben's "confession" had saved him from the much harsher sentence that he undoubtedly deserved.

Music and Murder

Violet Berling

On the morning of October 12, 1950, police in Long Beach, California received a call from a frantic woman. The caller identified herself as Violet John Berling, a music teacher. One of her students, she said, had collapsed and was unresponsive. The child did not appear to be breathing.

Obtaining the address from Berling, officers rushed to the scene. They expected to find the child lying on the floor or perhaps on a bed. But the small Long Beach apartment presented a rather more bizarre vista. Ten-year-old Katherine Frances Erickson was strapped into a straight-backed chair, her hands and feet tied. Her instrument of choice, an accordion, was still strapped around her shoulders and resting on her lap. When a police officer asked Berling who had placed the child in this position, she offered a bizarre response. The child had done it herself, she said. Lashing herself to furniture, was just one of her many strange habits. Thus began one of the strangest murder cases in the annals of Los Angeles county.

To understand the background against which this murder occurred one has to first take a small detour to the prevailing culture of the era. In the early 1950's the accordion was a very popular instrument. It wasn't at all uncommon for teens (and even pre-teens) to play in accordion ensembles. Accordion lessons were thus in demand and a small cottage industry grew to meet it, with teachers providing lessons out of their homes.

Katherine Erickson (known to her friends and family as Kay) was by all accounts a prodigy on the instrument. Her teacher, Violet Berling, was considered to be one of the best in the Long Beach area so it was unsurprising that Kay's parents chose her to provide their daughter with lessons. But the relationship went deeper than a teacher/student arrangement. Berling had confidently informed the Erickson's that she could turn their daughter into a star. When she asked that Kay be allowed to live with her in her Long Beach apartment, they agreed. They even consented to Berling's request that they shouldn't visit Kay. It would destroy the girl's focus, she said.

So how had it got to this? How had the lifeless body of the child prodigy ended up strapped to a chair? Berling had a ready explanation, even if few were prepared to believe it. According to the music teacher, Kay Erickson was possessed. She attributed this condition to the strange religious rituals observed by the child's parents. The Ericksons, she said, went to faith healing services and attended a church where one of the core beliefs was that "cosmic rays" were beamed down from copper wires on the chapel's ceiling. These practices had had a profound effect on the child. She believed that she had special powers and that she received instructions from her dead grandfather. Those instructions told her to inflict harm on herself. It was to prevent her from doing so that Berling had tied her to the chair.

To the detectives taking down this outlandish statement, the story sounded like the rantings of a lunatic. However, the autopsy would bear out at least some of Berling's testimony. The child had indeed been grievously harmed. Kay Erickson had died of asphyxiation after drowning on her own vomit. That, however, told only a small part of the story. The little girl had suffered horrendous and sustained abuse. Her body was covered with various wounds, some fresh, some of older vintage. Aside from bruises and abrasions, there were numerous thin cuts inflicted with a sharp instrument such as a razor blade. In addition, there were burn marks, some made with a lit cigarette, others bearing the unmistakable triangular shape of a clothes iron.

If that were not enough there was also evidence of sexual trauma. Both the vagina and anus were found to be dilated which, according to the medical examiner indicated frequent stretching with a foreign object over an extended period. As for Berling's assertion that any of this damage was self-inflicted, the M.E. declared that that was impossible. Someone had tortured this little girl to death and the only person who had had the opportunity to do that was Violet Berling. He also determined that Kay Erickson had been dead for at least five hours by the time Berling called the police.

Violet Berling was thus arrested and charged with murder, her trial date set for early 1951. And if the public thought that they had heard the last of the bizarre claims and counterclaims in the case they were mistaken. Despite all evidence to the contrary, Berling continued to insist that she had acted with Kay's best interests at heart. She admitted that she sometimes inflicted corporal punishment but only when Kay acted out and threw temper tantrums. She also confessed to sometimes tying Kay to a chair or to a filing cabinet but said that this was only to stop her harming herself. One time, she said, she'd come home to find the child burning her flesh with a clothes iron. When she'd asked Kay why she'd done it the little girl had replied: "Because it feels so good." Bizarrely, Berling also claimed that Kay sometimes tied herself to the chair because it improved her accordion playing.

Beatrice Erickson then took the stand and tearfully explained how her daughter had fallen into the hands of the music teacher. She said that her family often struggled financially. Her husband was in the Navy and was often away at sea. The money he sent was barely enough to pay the rent and feed her children. She had therefore had to cut back on expenses and had therefore told "Mrs. John" (Violet Berling's professional name) that she was going to have to cancel Kay's lessons. She just could not afford the $4 per month.

Berling, however, had urged her to let Kay continue with her lessons. She'd said that Kay was a prodigy who would go on to become a professional and make lots of money, but only if Mrs. Erickson entrusted the child to her care for "proper training and tuition." That meant that Kay would move in with Berling and her family would not be allowed to visit her. Mrs. Erickson would not even be allowed to attend recitals, which Berling said were "private affairs." Wanting the best for her daughter, Mrs. Erickson had naively agreed to the arrangement.

Throughout Beatrice Erickson's testimony, Violet Berling had been putting on quite a show for the court. She sighed, sobbed uncontrollably, pulled at her hair and sometimes fell into a dead faint, forcing the judge to call a recess. But her behavior was to become even more extreme once a succession of her former pupils took to the stand to describe her abuse of Kay and also the mistreatment they had suffered at her hands.

A 9-year-old who played in an accordion quartet with Kay, said that she saw Kay with bandages wrapped around her face on at least four occasions, with only the eyes and nose exposed. She said that the music teacher once took a group of students to watch a movie. Kay was among them but the little girl was required to sit through the entire production with a scarf covering her eyes so that she couldn't see. She said that she'd seen Berling kick Kay and the teacher had also instructed other children to kick her. Other children reported seeing Kay tied up and forced to sit in a narrow gap behind a sofa.

Other testimony was even more sickening. According to one child, Kay had been forced by Berling to sit in front of a group of children and masturbate. Berling had then threatened them with punishment if they said anything to their parents. This same child said that he hoped his music teacher went to the gas chamber. Listening to this, Berling had another of her "spells" and had to be removed from the courtroom while the trial continued.

But Berling was present when the matter was eventually handed over to the jury. The trial had lasted all of four months and was at the time one of the longest in California history. And the jury deliberations would be similarly protracted. After eight days, they eventually returned to find Violet Berling guilty of first degree murder. Berling collapsed in tears when the verdict was announced. (The jury foreman would later say that they had all agreed within 30 minutes that Berling was guilty. The rest of the time was taken up by discussion centered on the degree of guilt.)

Violet Berling was sentenced to life in prison. The matter, of course, went on appeal and the defense had a valid argument for having the case reheard. Under California law at the time, a defendant had to be present at every stage of a felony prosecution. Since Berling's frequent fainting spells had kept her out of the courtroom, her appeal was granted. This time she opted to waive her right to a jury trial and have the matter heard by a judge. But she fared no better. Found guilty, she was sentenced to life in prison with parole eligibility in seven years. The minimum term was later increased by the California Parole Board to fifty years.

False Evidence

On the afternoon of Sunday, October 7, 1994, 9-year-old Daniel Handley was riding his bicycle on the Beckton council estate in London, England. The day was frigid, with a stiff, arctic breeze and ominous overhanging cloud bringing an early twilight. Still, Daniel was in no hurry to get home. Life in the apartment he shared with his mother and four brothers was nobody's idea of fun, especially since his mother's latest boyfriend had moved in. Alex Joseph was none too quick with his brain but plenty quick with his fists. The boys lived in terror of him and spent as much time as they could away from the family home.

Daniel had just turned onto Tollgate Road when he noticed a silver Peugeot 305 parked at the curb. There was a man at the wheel, another hunkered over the hood trying to keep a large sheet of paper from being ripped away by the breeze. Despite the coldness of the day, the rear passenger door stood wide open. As Daniel approached, the man standing outside the vehicle turned and gave him a smile. "Can you help us out here, mate?" he asked. It was then that Daniel saw that the sheet of paper he was holding was a map.

Daniel Handley was an independent and streetwise young boy who was already making his own way in life. He worked as a trolley-jockey at the local ASDA supermarket, he washed windshields at traffic lights, he delivered pamphlets, he did odd jobs around the estate, anything to make a buck. The money was spent on fast food, comic books and cigarettes. Sometimes he even had enough to buy clothes, like the red sweater he was wearing on this particular day, the word "Champion" emblazoned across the front of it. Now, he skidded his bike to a stop and sized up the man holding the map. Daniel was naturally wary of strangers but he was always on the lookout for ways to make money. Perhaps there might be a tip in this for him. Lowering his bicycle to the tarmac, he walked over.

The man holding the map was named Brett Tyler. He was a 29-year-old Londoner, born a few minutes away from the Beckton Estate in Limehouse. These days, though, he worked as a controller for a taxi service named Guy's Cars in Bristol, where he was currently putting in extra shifts so that he could return to his adopted home in the Philippines. He was also a convicted pedophile who sometimes posed as a priest in order to lure young children.

The man sitting behind the wheel of the car was also a convicted sex offender. If anything, he was worse than Tyler, having served prison time for raping young boys. Thirty-one-year-old Tim Morss was from Islington, north London, although he lived these days in

Bristol where he ran a flower shop called Green Fingers. He also worked part-time as a taxi-driver for Guy's Cars, which was operated by his gay lover, 58-year-old David Guttridge. Morss and Tyler had come out to the estate that day looking for a blond-haired boy of about nine or ten. Daniel Handley fit the bill perfectly.

Morss and Tyler's abduction plan, however, were about to hit a snag. While Tyler was talking to Daniel, a Moroccan man was driving with his family along Tollgate Road. The man did not know Daniel Handley but the scene before him looked suspicious. Here was a man talking to little boy while his friend sat behind the wheel of the car staring straight ahead. And why was the back door standing open? The man drove on to the traffic circle halfway down the road and then decided to loop around and check it out. As he approached the Peugeot, he deliberately slowed his vehicle so that he could eyeball the men talking to the boy. And his suspicions appeared to be confirmed when the men jumped into their car and raced off. The man then drove home, confident that they had chased off the strangers and quite possibly prevented a crime from being committed.

But the men in the Peugeot were not gone. Morss and Tyler had spent much of this filthy day hunting for the right boy and they were not about to give up now. Daniel had barely reached the traffic circle when he saw the silver car come racing back towards him. This time, there was no attempt at finesse. The door was flung open and one of the men jumped from the vehicle. After a brief struggle, Daniel was forced into the back seat. Then the car raced off again, leaving Daniel's red bicycle by the roadside.

Just over four hours later, at around 10:45 pm, Maxine Handley called the police to report that her nine-year-old son, Daniel, was missing. The case was assigned to Detective Superintendent Ed Williams, a veteran of the force who had cut his teeth working under the legendary investigator, "Nipper" Read, on the "Babes in the Wood" murder case. Since then, DS Williams had gained a degree in psychology and had built a reputation as an accomplished detective in his own right. He had a nose for where a case was going and this one bothered him. Right from the start, he believed that Daniel had been abducted by a pedophile gang and those fears were given credence three days later when a couple of estate boys came forward to hand in Daniel's bicycle. They'd found it abandoned at the side of Tollgate Road, they said.

DS Williams' first step in the investigation was to appeal to the public. And as always happens in these cases, the appeal produced a deluge of well-intentioned but false information. There was, however, one useful lead. The Moroccan man came forward to report what he'd seen and was able to provide a description of the abductors and their vehicle. This information was then aired on the BBC program Crimewatch and delivered 138 tips, all of them useless.

While all of this was going on, DS Williams was following another investigative strategy, this one dealing with the very real possibility that Daniel had been murdered. Divers were sent to the bottoms of rivers, docks, and tidal basins; officers searched wasteland, warehouses and parkland; detectives started calling on known pedophiles in the area. Nothing. Daniel Handley had apparently vanished into thin air.

The police were not without avenues of inquiry, though. For a time, the investigation focused strongly on Daniel's family. Bizarre and disturbing stories had reached the ears of the investigators – about how group sex sessions took place at their home; about how local children visited the house to spy on Maxine Handley and her lover while they were having sex; about how Handley and Joseph knew about this and didn't care.

Alex Joseph, in particular, worried DS Williams. Tall and powerfully built, he had an IQ of just 70 and a notoriously short-temper. He'd once confided to a counsellor that he sometimes had fantasies about killing children. He had also attacked Maxine's children in the past so was it possible that he'd taken things further this time and killed Daniel? Was it possible that Maxine was covering for him? It was a possibility that could not be ignored.

Maxine Handley and Alex Joseph were taken into custody on December 14, 1994. But despite hours of rigorous questioning they steadfastly denied any involvement in Daniel's disappearance. Williams believed Maxine but he wasn't that sure about Alex Joseph. He therefore brought in a psychiatrist to examine Joseph, with the therapist concluding that Joseph was too dim-witted to have concocted a cover story, let alone being able to stick to it under interrogation. He had trouble remembering and reciting back the days of the week. Joseph and Maxine Handley were released soon after. The investigation was back to square one.

Over the next three months the police leaned heavily on their network of informants, including several known pedophiles, in their efforts to track down Daniel Handley and his abductors. DS Williams's greatest fear was that Daniel was being held somewhere as a sex slave and that every day that passed was another day of suffering for the boy. Then, six months after Daniel's disappearance, came the break, but not the outcome, that Williams had been praying for.

On March 27, 1995, a man was walking his dog on the outskirts of Bradley Stoke, a small town just north of Bristol. As the dog chased rabbits through the undergrowth, the man spotted what he at first thought an old bicycle helmet. Closer inspection however, revealed that it was skull, with the size suggesting that it was from a child. The man then ran to the clubhouse of a nearby golf course and called the police.

Detectives and a crime scene unit were on site within the hour. Carefully cutting back the undergrowth, they discovered a red sweater with the word "Champion" across it. This detail had been widely circulated in the Handley investigation and so the lead detective immediately called DS Williams. Dental records would later prove that the skull and the 26 small bones buried nearby belonged to the missing boy.

The prospect of finding Daniel alive was now gone but that only made Ed Williams and his team more determined than ever to catch the person or persons who had taken him and ended his life. Now, at least, they had something to work on. Thus far, their investigation had been focused on London. Was it possible that their perpetrator was from Bristol and had brought Daniel up here? In order to test that theory, Williams turned again to Crimewatch, appealing for anyone who might have seen Daniel in the Bristol area to come forward. He was soon rewarded with a couple of promising leads.

One witness reported seeing a boy who looked like Daniel being pulled unwillingly along a Bristol street by two men. Another said that she had been with her daughter at Paul's Cafe in Thornbury several months earlier and had seen a boy who resembled Daniel sitting with three men. One of the men in particular, had stuck in her memory. He was heavy-set and muscular, "a bull of a man," as she described him.

Williams believed that this lead was particularly promising. However, he needed every scrap of detail that the witness could recall. In order to extract it, he asked the witness if she'd be prepared to take part in a re-enactment of the scene. The woman immediately agreed.

The plan, however, soon hit a snag. Paul's Café had closed down and the site it had occupied had been stripped of all furniture and fittings. Undeterred, Williams got in a team to reconstruct the location, working from photographs. He then brought in his witness and had her and her daughter follow the same route they'd taken to the café that day, park in the same spot, order the same meal. It was unconventional but it worked. The woman was able to vividly recall the day and more importantly, the "bull of a man," she'd seen. Williams felt strongly that this was his prime suspect. But who was he? He turned again to Crimewatch to find out. And again his efforts were rewarded.

The same night that the picture was shown, Williams garnered his most valuable clue to date. A psychiatrist thought that it resembled one of his patients, a man who had confided his fantasy of abducting, raping and murdering a boy of Daniel's age. Psychiatrists are, of course, bound by doctor/patient confidentiality but not where they have information that might prevent the commission of a crime. And if this man, who had described his fantasy in such graphic detail, had actually followed through and killed a boy, then there was every likelihood that he would strike again. The psychiatrist therefore contacted DS Williams and gave up his patient's name. He was particularly concerned, be explained, because this man lived in the area where Daniel's body had been found. His name was Tim Morss.

The investigation quickly gained momentum after that. Williams began looking into Morss' background; he saw that Morss closely resembled the man described by his eyewitness; he learned that Morss had previous convictions for child abuse; he noted Morss's familiarity with the area from which Daniel had been abducted. Moreover, Morrs lived in Bradley Stoke, where Daniel's body had been found.

Tim Morss was taken into custody on May 30, along with his lover, David Guttridge. Gutteridge would later be absolved of involvement in the murder, although he'd be charged as an accessory after the fact. In the meantime, he'd given up the name of Morss's accomplice, Brett Tyler. Tyler had since fled to the Philippines but he was arrested there two weeks later and extradited to the UK. There he quickly began talking, revealing the horrific details of Daniel Handley's death.

According to Tyler, he and Morss had long fantasized about kidnapping a blond-haired little boy, raping him and then killing him. He explained how they'd driven down to London on that October day with exactly that in mind, how they had almost abandoned their mission after being spotted by the Moroccan man; how they'd decided to follow through anyway. Daniel had been taken to an apartment above the premises of Guy's Cars in Bristol. There, Tyler kept him captive while Morss went to fetch his video camera. He wanted to keep a record of his vile deeds. When Morss returned, he and Tyler took turns raping the boy while the other operated the camera. They then told Daniel to get dressed and said that they were taking him home. Instead they drove to an isolated spot near Bradley Stoke, stopping off at the home of Brett Tyler's father to pick up a garden fork and a spade. Daniel Handley was strangled to death by Morss, using a tow rope. They then buried him in a shallow grave.

It was an incredible story but one that DS Williams fully believed. After all, it closely matched the evidence. Or did it? One striking exception stood out. If Morss and Tyler had killed Daniel within six hours of abducting him (and the police had no reason to disbelieve them) then the boy who the eyewitness had seen in Paul's Café could not have been Daniel. The vital, case-breaking clue had been incorrect. Nonetheless this "false clue" had ended the careers of two vile pedophiles and DS Williams would be eternally grateful for that.

Timothy Morss and Brett Tyler were brought to trial at the Old Bailey on May 17, 1996. Found guilty of murder they were sentenced to life imprisonment, with the recommendation that they should never be released.

Murder, Miami-Style

Joyce Lemay Cohen

"Greed is good," that famous line, uttered by Michael Douglas' character in the award winning "Wall Street" has often been cited as a catchword for the eighties. And it is not that far from the mark. The decade does seem, in retrospect, to have been one endless party, when money was plentiful and the pursuit of it was considered the greatest of American virtues. Miami real estate tycoon, Stanley Cohen, certainly seemed to live by that credo. In the game of wealth accumulation, there were few in South Florida to match him.

Cohen was not a Florida native. Born in 1934, he was the eldest of four children of a New York City furrier. He grew up on Long Island, but moved with his family to Florida in 1948, when he was 14. After graduating from Miami High School three years later, he attended the University of Florida, where he earned a degree in civil engineering and the nickname 'Crusher.' Thereafter, he accepted a junior management position with a construction firm.

He also got married for the first time, a union that would produce two children, Gary and Gerri.

Stan Cohen was an ambitious man. In 1963, at the age of just 29 and with a young family to feed, he gave up his cushy corporate job and struck out on his own, founding SAC Construction (after Stanley Alan Cohen). And his timing could not have been better. The Sunshine State was entering an unprecedented boom that would see its population double over the next two decades. Demand for housing and associated facilities was huge and Cohen was uniquely positioned to take advantage of it. His company was soon inundated with work and gained a solid reputation as a builder of shopping malls, medical facilities and other business premises. He also got a number of state and federal commissions for the construction of government buildings. Still not satisfied with the amount of work coming his way, he branched out into residential real estate development. The work was hard and the hours long but the rewards were great. Before long Stanley Cohen was a multi-millionaire.

But the demands of his workaholic lifestyle were taking a toll on Cohen's family life. His first marriage fell apart and so too did the next two he embarked on. Not that Cohen seemed to mind. He wasn't a handsome man by any stretch of the imagination but he was seldom without female companionship. Money, as they say, is the ultimate aphrodisiac.

In the fall of 1974, Stanley Cohen was engaged to a woman who was shortly to become his fourth wife. But all of those plans were swept aside when Stan walked into an office at one of his construction sites and spotted a petite brunette who had just been hired as a secretary. Her name was Joyce Lemay McDillon and Stan decided there and then, that he had to have her. Within days he had broken off his engagement. A few weeks later, on December 5, 1974, he and Joyce tied the knot in an opulent affair at the Dunes Hotel in Las Vegas. The groom was 40 years old at the time, his bride a sprightly 24.

The new Mrs. Cohen had arrived in Florida by a very different path to her husband. She had been born poor in Carpentersville, Illinois, a city of some 30,000 inhabitants on the northwest edge of Chicago. Her father, Bonnie Lemay, was a Native American, while her mother, Eileen Wojtanek, was of Polish extraction. If was a tough childhood with both parents frequently out of work due to their drinking problems and Bonnie not averse to using his fists on his wife. Eventually, Eileen had had enough. She split, taking Joyce with her. Over the years that followed she'd bounce from one abusive relationship to the next, all the while sinking deeper and deeper into the bottle.

In 1964, Joyce was sent to live with her aunt, Bea Wojtanek, back in Carpentersville. She would remain under her aunt's roof for the next four years until, at 17, she became pregnant by a local boy, George McDillon. The couple married and had a son, Shawn, nine months later. Thereafter they set up house together and George worked as a drywall installer, while Joyce did secretarial work. The next five years would be fraught with financial problems. George was a hard worker but his meager salary was no match for his wife's expensive tastes. When Joyce convinced him to move to Florida to take advantage of the building boom there, he was willing to listen, if only to make some inroads into the couple's mounting debt. But George failed to settle in Florida and within a year he was back in Carpentersville. Joyce stayed behind with Shawn. Soon after, she'd snared Stanley Cohen. The life of want that she had known thus far was about to take a sharp turn for the better.

Joyce Cohen adapted to the role of wealthy socialite with ease. Soon she was cruising around town in a white Jaguar, moving into a landmark Coral Rock mansion overlooking Biscayne Bay, clubbing at Miami's trendiest nightspots, eating at the best restaurants, shopping at the most expensive boutiques. Stan adopted her 5-year-old son, and paid for the interior design course she wanted to take. The skills she acquired were put to use expensively refurnishing their home. There were vacations in the Bahamas, Ocho Rios, Jamaica, Las Vegas and Cancun, Mexico and there was the 600-acre ranch that they acquired in Steamboat Springs, Colorado. Of course, regular trips between Florida and Colorado necessitated Stan buy his own corporate jet. To someone who had grown up as dirt poor as Joyce Cohen, it must have appeared a compelling approximation of heaven on earth.

But by the mid-eighties, cracks had begun to appear in the perfect façade of the Cohens' marriage. Both Stan and Joyce had developed cocaine habits and Stan's famously wandering eye had driven him into the arms of a former lover, something that apparently infuriated Joyce even though she was having an affair herself. When the couple were together at their Coral Rock home, they slept in separate bedrooms. More often though, they were in different states, Stan in Florida and Joyce in Colorado. There she confided to friends – including country singer Tanya Tucker – that she wanted out of her marriage. She even remarked to one acquaintance that she wished Stanley were dead. After eleven years of marriage, Joyce had come to the conclusion that, while she wanted the lifestyle that Stan's money afforded her, she no longer wanted Stan.

At 5:25 a.m. on March 7, 1986, a hysterical woman called 911 in Miami and told the dispatcher that her husband had been shot in their Coconut Grove home. The police arrived to find 52-year-old Stanley Cohen lying naked on his bed, dead from three gunshot wounds to the head, his wife Joyce clearly distressed. After an officer managed to calm her down, she told them what she knew. She had been working on a charity project in one of the downstairs bedrooms, she said, when she'd heard a loud noise. She'd gone up to investigate, taking her pet Doberman Pinscher with her. As she was climbing the stairs she had seen two men running out of the house. She'd then entered the master bedroom and found her husband dead.

On the face of it, Joyce Cohen's story had a ring of truth about. At around this time there had been a spate of home invasions in the city and Miami PD had yet to apprehend the culprits. But if the killers had entered the home intent on robbery, why had they fled empty-handed? The mansion was filled with fine furnishings, and the intruders might have found cash and other valuables if they'd bothered to look. No, this certainly did not appear to be a home invasion gone wrong. And that left only one other possibility – a hit on Stanley Cohen.

This too, was not beyond the realms of possibility. For years now there had been talk that Stan Cohen had been associating with underworld types. There were even rumors that he was using his private jet to smuggle cocaine. Is that what this was? A professional hit? At this early stage of the investigation it seemed like an avenue worth pursuing.

But then Joyce Cohen did something that would turn the focus of the inquiry firmly in her direction. When detectives asked for permission to search the house, she refused and ordered them to vacate the premises immediately. Investigators were forced to get a search warrant, a delay of eight hours during which they had no access to the crime scene. When they were eventually allowed in, they determined that three .38 caliber bullets had penetrated the victim's skull, while a fourth shot had grazed his scalp. The murder weapon was found later that afternoon in a stand of ferns in the Cohens' yard. It was a Smith & Wesson revolver, registered to Stanley Cohen. Fragments of tissue-paper were found stuck to the trigger guard, apparently used by the shooter to remove fingerprints. A similar tissue was found in a wastebasket in Joyce's bedroom. It contained gun residue.

And further problems with Joyce's version of events soon emerged. According to her, she'd heard the shots at just after 5 a.m. But a neighbor had also heard gunfire. He claimed that it was around 3 a.m. and that fit the medical examiner's estimated time of death. So what was Joyce Cohen doing during those missing two hours? Why had she waited so long before calling 911?

Joyce wasn't saying. Instead she lawyered-up, hiring one of Florida's top (and most expensive) defense attorneys, Alan Ross. His first step was to arrange a lie-detector test for his client, which she passed on the second attempt. Meanwhile, civil suits were coming thick and fast. First, Stanley Cohen's children from his first marriage, Gary Cohen and Gerri Helfman, filed a $5 million wrongful death lawsuit against Joyce. She responded with an $11 million suit of her own, for slander. While all of this was going on, the case that really mattered, the criminal prosecution for murder, had ground to a halt. The D.A. simply did not have enough evidence to successfully prosecute a case against Joyce Cohen.

Days, weeks and months passed without criminal charges being filed. Then, out of the blue, came a break in the case. The source was hardly a paragon of truth and virtue. Frank Zuccarello was a member of a gang who specialized in home invasion robberies. While being held pending his latest court date, Zuccarello contacted Miami detectives with an interesting piece of intel to share. He said that he knew who had killed Stanley Cohen.

Over a series of interviews, Zuccarello revealed to detectives that Joyce Cohen had hired him and two accomplices, Thomas Joslin and Anthony Caracciolo, to kill her husband. She had provided the murder weapon and a sketch of the house, guiding them to Stanley's bedroom. She had also turned off the alarm system, and ensured that her pet Doberman was locked up, making it easy for them to enter, carry out the hit and leave. Caracciolo had been the trigger-man, according to Zuccarello, and the payoff had been $100,000 worth of cocaine.

This was an interesting piece of information and one that the authorities had not anticipated. Detectives had believed all along that Joyce had pulled the trigger herself. Nonetheless, it had to be looked into and so investigators visited Joslin and Caracciolo in jail and subjected both of them to a vigorous round of interrogation. Despite both men insisting that they'd had nothing to do with the murder, both were charged in September 1988. Now it was time to track down the main focus of the investigation, Joyce Cohen. They found her in Chesapeake, Virginia where she was living in a trailer park with her new boyfriend, Robert Dietrich. The halcyon days of Caribbean vacations and skiing trips to Colorado were well and truly behind her.

Joyce Lemay Cohen went on trial in Miami in the fall of 1989. The early part of the prosecution's case focused mainly on her many and frequent complaints about Stan and how she wished to be free of him. The star witness though, was Frank Zuccarello, who despite his background, came across as lucid and believable. It was likely his testimony that convinced the jurors. After a trial lasting three weeks, they took less than a day to return a guilty verdict against Joyce Cohen. Judge Fredericka Smith then imposed a life sentence. Anthony Caracciolo and Thomas Joslin subsequently agreed to plead no contest to second-degree murder and were given reduced sentences, while Frank Zuccarello received immunity and was free by the time the other three accused went on trial.

But the Cohen case did not end there. In 1998, Miami reporter, Gail Bright, revealed that Jon Spear, the lead investigator on the case, had told her confidentially that he knew Caracciolo and Joslin were not involved. He had always believed that Joyce had pulled the trigger herself but lacked the evidence to prove it. Zuccarello's story, although a lie, had been the only way to put her behind bars.

These revelations, of course, sparked a clamor for a new trial but the motion was ultimately rejected. Joyce Cohen is currently incarcerated at Broward Correctional Institution in Fort Lauderdale, where she is inmate No. 161701. Her earliest parole date is April 2048. She will be 97 years old by then.

To Kill a Witch

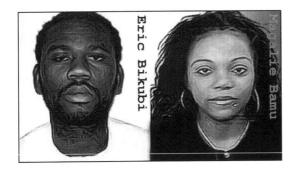

Fifteen-year-old Kristy Bamu was looking forward to spending Christmas in London with his older sister Magalie. The soccer-mad youngster had always been fascinated by the English capital and its famous football clubs, Chelsea, Arsenal and West Ham. And he was equally keen to meet his sister's boyfriend, Eric Bikubi, who coached a junior soccer team. He was eager to sit down with the older man to talk tactics, formations and favorite players. Maybe he could pick up some tips to improve his game. Maybe Eric would even take him to watch a Premier League match.

Also accompanying Kristy on that Christmas vacation in 2010 were his brother Yves, sister Kelly, and two younger siblings aged 11 and 13. The group had traveled from their home in Paris, France via Eurostar and arrived in London on December 22. They were met at London St. Pancras station by Magalie and Eric. Thereafter, they took the tube to Newham, where the couple had their home. Kristy was enthralled by the buzz of the city he'd so long wanted to visit but he had to admit that he was a bit disappointed by Eric and Magalie's living conditions. Their apartment was pokey and cold and there were tools, boxes of floor tiles and bags of cement stacked against the walls and dust everywhere. "We're making some improvements," Magalie explained.

But it was Eric who most mystified the impressionable teen. His father had told him that Magalie's boyfriend was "a good man, a kind man." He'd expected to be welcomed with open arms. Why then did Eric appear so hostile? Why was he just standing there, glaring at his guests? Kristy wondered what he might have done to offend this man who he'd only just met. It was probably nothing serious, he decided eventually. Eric was probably just one of those guys who was slow to warm to strangers.

But as the day progressed, Kristy became more and more concerned about Eric's behavior. The man was hardly making an effort to welcome his house guests. He spoke barely a word and responded to any attempts at conversation with a grunt. Not only that but his eyes seemed to burn with a barely concealed rage. Several times Kristy felt the heat of that glare and, quite frankly, it frightened him. He could not, however, have anticipated the reason for Eric's animosity.

That evening, the group was sitting around in the dusty living room making awkward conversation which neither Eric nor Magalie chose to participate in. Kristy, who had eaten nothing since noon, was starving. Their hosts had offered nothing to eat or drink all day, not even a cup of tea. Several times, Kristy had thought to chirp in with a cheeky, "What's for dinner?" just as he would at home. But a glare from Eric dissuaded him from that course. So terrified was he of the man that he dared not even walk towards the bathroom even though he desperately needed to relieve himself. Now, as Kristy contemplated his rumbling tummy and overfull bladder, Eric finally broke his silence.

"What have you brought into my house?" he demanded of his guests, his voice beginning in a whisper and terminating in a scream that so terrified Kristy that his bladder released. Then, as the dark patch spread across the front of Kristy's jeans, Eric started sniffing furiously at the air, his nose twitching like a bloodhound who had just picked up a particularly interesting scent. "Witch," he hissed. Then, without warning, he sprang from his seat, snatched up a hammer and crossed the floor rapidly towards Kristy. The boy barely had time to react when the hammer came at him in an arc, colliding with his teeth and loosening them in a spray of blood. "You're all witches!" Eric screamed. "All of you!"

For a moment, nobody in the apartment had time to react. Then Yves stepped forward, only to be backed off by the hammer. Kelly turned towards her sister but found no solace there. Magalie had taken on the same wild-eyed, flared-nostril stance as her boyfriend. Kristy, meanwhile, stood clutching his damaged mouth while blood seeped between his fingers. The two younger children had backed into a corner and stood clutching each other and whimpering quietly. That was how it started.

To most Westerners, witches and witchcraft are a relic of the ignorant, superstitious Middle Ages. But in certain cultures, particularly in Africa, witchdoctors exert a very real influence on people's daily lives. Many rely of them for healing and for advice on matters of finance, love, and luck. They can also be called on to place curses on rivals or to lift hexes.

These, however, are not the sort of witches that Eric Bikubi was referring to when he made his accusation against the Bamus. The kind he was talking about operate under the radar, and often require human body parts (usually obtained by murder) for their "spells." When a community suspects the activities of these malevolent witches, they will often hire a specialist "witch smeller" to point out the individuals concerned. And anyone thus identified has little chance of survival. Most often they are summarily burned, beaten, or hacked to death by a baying mob. We've seen this quite recently in Tanzania and Nigeria, and we've seen it in the Congo in 1999, when most of the victims were children.

Eric Bikubi, as we have already noted, was born in the Congo, where a form of witchcraft known as Kindoki is practiced. There is no evidence to suggest that he was ever trained as a "witch sniffer" but it appears that he regarded himself as a talented amateur. Even before that fateful Christmas of 2010, he had accused several people in the local Congolese community of being witches. Now, it appears, he'd set his sights on his girlfriend's family.

On December 23, Pierre Bamu, the family patriarch, received a call from Bikubi, instructing him to fetch his children. "They're all witches," he spat, "and you're a witch too. If they remain in my house, they will die." Bikubi then put Kristy on the line and the boy beseeched his father to travel to London and pick them up.

Tragically, Pierre did not heed the request. Kristy had not sounded at all distressed over the phone and so Pierre put the whole incident down to a family spat that would soon be resolved. It wasn't. In fact, by the time that Bikubi made that call, he'd already embarked on a campaign of torture that would resolve ultimately in murder.

Over the next three days, the Bamus were held prisoner in the tiny apartment by their sister and her boyfriend. Each was tortured in turn, their tormentors using whatever implements were at hand. A hammer, metal poles, pliers, chisels, the sharp edges of ceramic tiles. They were not given anything to eat or drink, not allowed to sleep. Instead they were badgered night and day to confess their offense. "Admit that you are witches and submit to the deliverance ceremony," Eric told them. "That is the only way you will be free."

Given the option between confessing to an imaginary wrong and suffering torture, it is no surprise that the Bamus relented – first the children, then Yves and then Kelly. But Kristy would not relent. He was not a witch and he refused to confess to being one.

And so 15-year-old Kristy suffered the worst of the beating. His teeth were pounded from his skull with a hammer and chisel, his ears were ripped with pliers, he was beaten over the head with steel bars, his skin was ripped with ceramic tiles. It was Eric who inflicted most of the torture but he was ably assisted by Magalie. And after the others "confessed" to being witches, Eric enlisted their help in beating and tormenting Kristy too, in order to prove that they were truly repentant. Afraid of what would happen if they refused, they joined in the torture of their brother.

By the frigid Christmas Day of 2010, Kristy had been so badly
beaten that he was barely able to stand. He was in so much pain
that he begged his sister and Eric to let him die. Those pleas fell on
deaf ears. Instead, Eric decided that despite Kristy's refusal to
admit his sins, it was time to move on to the "deliverance
ceremony." This involved herding the five siblings into the bathtub
and hosing them down with cold water from the shower head.
When Kristy fell and couldn't get up again, his brothers and sisters
were instructed to leave him be. When the water rose and covered
his mouth and nostrils, Eric and Magalie watched impassively. By
the time Eric pulled him from the water, Kristy was already dead.
Paramedics were then summoned via a 999 call. They arrived to
find the four surviving siblings huddled together, hysterical,
terrified and soaking wet. Each of them would be treated for shock
and minor cuts and abrasions. For Kristy, however, it was too late.
He had suffered 130 different injuries before drowning in the
bathtub.

Magalie Bamu and Eric Bikubi were arrested at the scene and
charged with murder. At trial, each tried to mitigate their
involvement in Kristy's death. Magalie claimed that she was
entirely under Eric's influence and afraid of what he would do to
her if she dared to disobey him. But her sister Kelly put paid to
that defense. She testified that Magalie had been a willing
participant and even, in some cases, the instigator of the violence.
"She said we deserved it," Kelly said. "I am sure she still believes
that we are witches. She had no pity for us and so I have no pity for
her."

Eric Bikubi, meanwhile, was falling back on the diminished responsibility defense. He claimed that he was schizophrenic, even though he'd never been diagnosed with the disease and court appointed psychiatrists could find no evidence to support a diagnosis. In the end, the jury rejected the defense and found him guilty. He was sentenced to life in prison with a minimum term of 30 years. Magalie Bamu also got life, her minimum term was set at 25 years.

But spare a thought for the Bamu family. A beloved son was gone, taken on the cusp of manhood over a superstitious belief that should have died out in the Middle Ages. Except that it hasn't died out. There are still those who believe in witches and witchcraft, even in modern societies. Over the last decade, Scotland Yard has investigated nearly 100 cases of ritualistic or faith-based abuse. Seventeen of those cases have resulted in murder convictions.

Warning! May Cause Death

John Kmetz was not a man who had a particular lust for life. Ever since his beloved wife had passed away a few years earlier, the 52-year-old landscape gardener had suffered from periods of depression so deep that he was often left debilitated and bedridden. Often he'd sit and contemplate his own death. But for his responsibility towards his two teenaged children, he might well have helped the process along.

But if there was one thing that at least helped Kmetz to cope with his adversity, it was his religious faith. Kmetz was a staunch Seventh Day Adventist and attended a church close to his home in East Los Angeles. It was through the church that he met 32-year-old spinster Esther Dockham, a teacher who gave classes at the church school. Esther too was lonely and in September 1940, she and John Kmetz began keeping company.

It wasn't a romantic attachment as such, at least not overtly. But the couple appeared to enjoy each other's company and Esther was good with the children. Often, the four of them would make a day trip to Hollywood to visit Esther's mother. The senior Mrs. Dockham appeared to approve of her daughter's well-mannered beau. All that was left was for John to pop the question.

And apparently he did, early in 1941. That was when Esther contacted her friends, Eva and Oscar Albertson, and told them that John had proposed. The Albertsons were delighted that Esther had at last found someone, and a church-going man at that. They too were devout Seventh Day Adventists although they attended a church near their home in San Pedro and didn't know John Kmetz. Nonetheless, they wished Esther well and said that they looked forward to meeting her fiance.

Before that meeting could occur, however, there appears to have been a breakdown in the engagement. In April 1941, Esther fired off a letter ending the relationship. "Personally I care nothing for you," it read. "I never have, and I never can." She went on to say that: "I don't care anything about you and I do not find pleasure anymore in being with you. It's been almost like a punishment for me the last few times..."

A few days after sending that cruel letter, Esther perhaps thought better of it and sent another, this one couched in gentler terms. The message, however, was the same. It was over between them.

There is no record of whether John ever responded to these letters, whether he tried to talk Esther around. Given his propensity for melancholia, it is far more likely that he took it as yet another disappointment in his wretched life. In any case, he did not see Esther at all until August when they bumped into each other at church camp in Lynwood. Then, he was surprised at her attitude. He had expected that she'd be standoffish but she appeared happy to see him. Before the camp was over, they'd agreed to meet up again a few days later. It was at that meeting that Esther explained the letters she'd sent. She said that she had sent it because she was afraid that all he saw in her was a housekeeper and mother for his children. John assured her that this was not the case, that he genuinely cared for her. Just days later, Esther sent the following postcard to her friends the Albertsons: "Dear Maw and Paw, Prepare for a shock. Mr. Kmetz and I are to be married Monday night!"

The wedding was a small affair. Esther's mother was too ill to attend and so the only guests were the Albertsons, John's kids and Esther's brother. Oscar Albertson gave the bride away and all agreed she looked radiant. Thereafter, the Kmetzes settled down to married life and they and the Albertsons became firm social friends. Esther seemed blissfully happy and confided in Eva Albertson that she was very much in love with John and didn't think that she could ever love another.

But two weeks after the wedding there was a frightening incident, one that the police would link to subsequent events. The Kmetz family had spent that Saturday visiting Esther's mother and had returned at around 10:30 p.m. Approaching their house, they spotted an older model car, similar to the one that Oscar Albertson drove. Thinking nothing of it, they parked and began offloading the groceries they'd bought on the way home. Esther and John's daughter then carried the provisions inside while John went to park the car in the detached garage behind the house. That was when the women heard a cry and the sound of a scuffle. Rushing outside, they'd found John crouched over nursing a minor head injury. He said that a man had jumped him, beaten him over the head and then run away when John fought back.

Shortly after the attack, a police cruiser was on patrol some four blocks from the Kmetz residence when the officers saw a vehicle run a stop sign and then race off at speed. The officers gave chase and found the vehicle abandoned about a half-mile away. Running the license plate revealed that the car was registered to Eva Albertson. Inside the vehicle, the patrolmen found a wallet containing the identity documents of Oscar Albertson. There was also a pair of eyeglasses...and a full set of clothes.

But that was not the only peculiar discovery of the night. Sometime between midnight and 1 a.m. the police found Oscar Albertson lying at the side of a road a mile from his car. He was dressed only in his underwear and socks and was holding his head, claiming he'd been attacked.

Albertson was taken to a nearby police station where he gave a bizarre statement. He claimed that he had received a postcard the previous day from a man named George Crocker, asking him to be at the cigar counter of the Vermont Jefferson Owl drug store at 8 o'clock that Saturday night. The letter offered a blacksmith job and since Albertson was a blacksmith, and unemployed at the time, he'd kept the appointment. Crocker, however, hadn't shown up. Albertson said that he'd left the drug store but had then decided to sit in his car for a few minutes. While he waited, a man approached and introduced himself as "Mr. O'Connor," an associate of Crocker. He apologized for Crocker's no show, saying that he'd had to work late at the local Sears-Roebuck store. He then suggested that they drive over there since Crocker finished work at 9 p.m. Then O'Connor asked a strange question. He asked if Albertson knew of a gardener looking for work. Albertson said that he did and gave him John Kmetz's details. The men then drove to meet Crocker.

The story already sounded unbelievable to the detectives listening in. But Albertson was only just getting started. After they met up with Crocker, he said, the two men forced him at gunpoint to drink liquor until he passed out. He'd only come to when the police officers had roused him.

The police were almost certain that Albertson had fabricated the story. What they didn't know was why? What was he hiding and was it in any way connected to the attack on John Kmetz? The police didn't think so. They were sure that the church-going Albertson had been caught up in some honey trap and had concocted the whole bizarre story to hide his indiscretion. But what then of his car, seen racing away from the Kmetz home soon after the attack? The police didn't know and frankly didn't care. No crime had been committed bar a minor assault. They had bigger fish to fry. One of those fish would soon be a rather unusual murder.

On the afternoon of October 10, 1941, John Kmetz was suffering with another of those depressive moods that so plagued him. That was perhaps because Esther was going away to spend the weekend with the Albertsons but by evening he'd perked up considerably. The following day, Saturday, he took his children to church as usual and appeared in good spirits. When he returned, he found a package and a letter on the front porch. The package came from the "Herb Specialty Company, 1436 N. Wilcox Ave., Hollywood, California." Carrying the package inside, Kmetz put it on a dresser in his bedroom. It remained there, unopened, until Esther returned on Sunday evening.

Later that night, as the couple was preparing for bed, Esther saw the package and remarked on it. John then opened the attached letter and read it out loud:

Dear Friend,

We are selecting a limited number of men in various localities in and about Los Angeles who have reached the age of forty or more whom we believe, without any hesitancy, need healthful help. This help is coming to you absolutely free of charge through the use of 'vitalizing vitamin vigor.' Please read this entire letter and then let these vitalizing vitamins put spring in your step.

Here is our plan. We are sending you, under separate cover, a ten days' supply of our 'vitalizing vitamin vigor' at no cost to you. Follow the simple directions carefully and when this supply is exhausted, if you are satisfied with the amazing results, send us ten names of men that you believe would be benefited by the use of 'vitalizing vitamin vigor' and for your trouble and benefit we will send you free of charge a 30-day supply. We believe this way is the best and cheapest advertising and a splendid method of helping each other including the other fellow.

It was signed "Dr. W.W. Mackelroy, Mgr."

Having read the letter, John then opened the package. Inside, separated into compartments, were twelve capsules, two dark in color the other ten light. According to the accompanying instructions, the dark capsules were to be taken before bed.

Kmetz picked up one of the dark capsules and rolled it over between his fingers. "You think I should take it?" he asked his wife.

Esther shrugged. "Why not?" she said. "I don't see that they could do any harm." Kmetz then carried the box of pills to the kitchen, poured himself a glass of water and, following the directions, swallowed one of the dark capsules.

The effect was almost immediate. Within a minute he was complaining of feeling dizzy. Then he collapsed on the bed, started breathing rapidly and groaning in pain. His eyes seemed to bulge, while foam began frothing up between his lips. Esther ran to call the family physician and he was soon on the scene and giving Kmetz something to induce vomiting. When that failed to work, he called for an ambulance. Before it arrived, John Kmetz was dead. Since it appeared obvious that Kmetz had been deliberately poisoned, the doctor then called the police.

Both the physician who treated Kmetz and the first police officer on the scene that night would later comment on Esther Kmetz's strange behavior. Given that her husband had just died a horrific death right in front of her, Esther was strangely calm, even joking with neighbors who had stopped by to support her. At one point she asked the doctor, "Is he is dead yet?" She also apparently tried to hide the letter that had accompanied the deadly pills. One of the officers had put it aside as evidence. Later, he found that it had been moved and discovered it in Esther's apron pocket.

John Kmetz's body was removed for autopsy where it was determined that the pill he'd swallowed had been laced with cyanide. It was later found that the poison had been obtained from a pesticide known as Cyanogas, a product freely available at any hardware store.

The police, meanwhile, had been following up on the letter that had accompanied the package. They soon had a clue. It appeared that 500 copies of the letter had been printed off on September 22 at a print shop in Santa Monica. The clerk who had taken the order thought that it might have been placed by a man who resembled Oscar Albertson. The manager of the shop was even more adamant. He said that he was 100% certain that it had been Albertson who had called on his establishment. Based on that identification, Albertson was arrested and charged with murder.

But the State of California had one serious flaw to its case. What possible reason did Albertson have to murder John Kmetz, a man he barely knew? The most obvious reason was sexual jealousy but try as they might the police were unable to find any hint of impropriety between Albertson and Esther Kmetz. Money could be easily ruled out since Kmetz was hardly well-off. And there was no indication that he had ever caused offense to anyone. Certainly, he'd never given anyone cause to kill him.

Nonetheless, the case went on and ended in a hung jury. Six weeks later, the state opted to put Albertson on trial again. By then, one of the key witnesses had disappeared. Esther Kmetz had dropped out of sight between the first trial and the second and despite a widespread search the police were unable to locate her. To this day, her whereabouts remain a mystery.

Esther Kmetz's testimony, however, would not be required to convict Albertson. After two handwriting experts both testified that it had been Albertson who had signed the "Herb Specialty Company" letter, the jury returned a unanimous guilty verdict.

It would be a short-lived conviction. Albertson had barely started his life term when the guilty verdict was overturned on appeal. The prosecutor then decided to abandon the case. It remains officially unsolved to this day.

So who killed John Kmetz and why? We will probably never know the definitive answer to those questions. There are, however, some clues that we can follow. After the trial, it emerged that the relationship between Oscar Albertson and Esther Kmetz might not have been as innocent as it appeared. There were various reports that Albertson's car had been spotted outside the school were Esther taught and outside her home. There was also an incident where someone had seen Esther and Albertson together and she had hastily introduced him as her 'uncle.' That is not to suggest that there was a sexual relationship between them but perhaps Albertson had a crush on Esther and could not countenance the idea of her in the arms of another man. That would certainly explain why John Kmetz was killed so soon after the wedding.

Or perhaps this enigmatic crime has an entirely different explanation. How, for example, do we explain Esther's strange behavior on the night of the murder? How do we explain her sudden disappearance? Was Esther killed to ensure her silence? Did she drop out of sight to avoid prosecution? We will never know. The murder of John Kmetz remains a fascinating (and frustrating) mystery.

Bus Ride to Hell

Vince Weiguang Li

Tim McLean was an easy guy to like. The handsome 22-year-old had a cheerful, outgoing personality, something that won him many friends and made him popular with the opposite sex. Not that Tim was ready to settle down just yet. He enjoyed his freedom and his job as a carnival worker.

On the evening of July 30, 2008, Tim was returning from a job in Edmonton, Alberta, riding a Greyhound to his home in Manitoba. It was a long haul, and already tired from his strenuous job, Tim took the opportunity to catch up on some shuteye. Sitting towards the back of the bus, one row in front of the washroom, he did not notice when the bus stopped in Erickson, Manitoba, at around 7:00 to let on a new passenger.

The man's name was Vince Weiguang Li, 40 years old, about 5-foot-8, and stoutly built. Li had been born in Dandong, China, and had immigrated to Canada in 2001, gaining citizenship in 2005.

But life had not been easy in his adopted country. Unable to find employment in his chosen field of software development, Li had worked at a number of menial jobs. For a time he delivered newspapers, then he flipped burgers at a McDonald's for minimum wage. All of this left Li deeply frustrated and put a tremendous strain on his marriage. In 2006, it ended in divorce.

On July 29, 2008, Li had asked his supervisor for a day off from his delivery job, so that he could attend an interview in Winnipeg. It was apparently for this reason that he'd boarded the eastbound bus at Ericson, taking a seat near the front. Later, after a scheduled stop, he gathered up his belongings and moved closer to the back, taking up a spot behind where Tim McLean sat dozing, headphones over his ears. As the bus rolled on into the night, Li sat staring straight ahead of him into the darkness. We don't know what was going through his mind. All we have to go on, is its bloody aftermath.

Just after 12 a.m., with the bus some 18 miles west of Portage La Prairie, a blood-curdling scream suddenly rang out. Passengers, many of them startled from sleep, sprang to their feet and turned towards the source of the commotion at the back of the bus. What they saw there took a moment to register. A Chinese man had a large knife and was plunging it repeatedly into the neck and chest of one of the other passengers, a slightly-built young man. The victim was trying to escape, but caught within the narrow confines between the seats, he had no chance. As the assailant continued his frenzied attack, the victim's attempts at defending himself grew weaker. Then he slumped back in the seat, mortally wounded. At this point, the assailant turned and glared back down the aisle, clutching a knife that was gleaming red with blood. All of this happened within a matter of mere seconds. Then pandemonium broke out on the bus as the passengers stampeded towards the exit, many of them screaming hysterically.

As the driver brought his vehicle to a shuddering halt and ushered his passengers quickly onto the hard shoulder of the highway, the attacker resumed his assault. He appeared now to be hacking at the corpse, cutting at it in a frenzied sawing motion. Then, to the horror of those standing beside the road, he held up the victim's severed head, displaying it to them like some grotesque trophy. That triggered fresh screams from the already traumatized passengers. Some even bent over and threw up into the dust. Others, including a burly trucker, were outraged and tried to board the bus to confront the attacker. But he came charging down the aisle at them, screeching and slashing wildly with his knife. Wisely, the trucker beat a retreat, and the driver then sealed the doors, locking the assailant inside. He, in turn, went back to the corpse and continued cutting at it. To the dismay of the onlookers he then bolted down several pieces of the victim's flesh.

By now, the Royal Canadian Mounted Police at Portage la Prairie had received a report of a stabbing aboard a Greyhound bus. Officers arrived at the scene to find the killer still on board, the passengers huddling by the roadside in obvious distress, some of them crying hysterically. Meanwhile, the killer stalked up and down the aisle like a caged beast, periodically returning to the corpse to cut off chunks of flesh and bolt them down. When the police instructed him to surrender, he shouted back: "I have to stay on the bus forever." The onsite officers then sent for a hostage negotiator and a tactical team. It looked like this was going to be a long night.

As the hours ticked away, the remaining passengers were taken on board another bus to Winnipeg while the standoff continued between the deranged killer and the police. Finally, at around 1:30 a.m., and with the SWAT team getting ready to move in, the killer made his move, kicking out the rear window and scrambling through it. He'd barely hit the ground when two darts from a Taser stopped him in his tracks and he was then quickly subdued and handcuffed. "I'm sorry. I'm guilty. Please kill me," he said as he was led to a waiting police cruiser. There, officers searched his pockets and turned up a macabre bounty – the victim's ears, nose, and tongue.

But there was even worse to come when the police boarded the bus. Tim McLean, the happy, pleasant guy who had only wanted to get home to his family, had been literally torn apart. Body parts were scattered throughout the vehicle. Some chunks of flesh had been neatly encased in plastic bags as though the killer had intended carrying them away with him. Other body parts, like the eyes and part of the heart, were missing. It appeared that they had been eaten.

The police by now knew the identity of the man they had in custody. But who was Vince Weiguang Li and why had he chosen to kill a total stranger in such a brutal way? If the police were looking for easy answers, there weren't any. Those who knew Li described him as a pleasant, hard-working man, whose only frustration was his inability to find work as a computer software engineer. Li had no record of mental illness, although there were some worrying signs in his background. His former wife said that he had "problems" although she had never known him to be violent. She said that he'd been hospitalized in 2003, after the Ontario Provincial Police found him walking along a highway and apparently disoriented. Asked where he was going, Li had told the officers that he was "following the sun as instructed by God." The former Mrs. Li also said that Vince often disappeared for long periods of time, took unexplained bus trips, and often had long conversations with himself.

Vince Weiguang Li went on trial in March 2009. The obvious defense strategy was to plead "not criminally responsible," the Canadian equivalent of "not guilty by reason of insanity." And that is exactly the strategy that Li's lawyer employed, bringing in an expert witness to testify that Li was suffering from paranoid schizophrenia. He had killed Tim McLean because the voice of God had told him to, the psychiatrist said. He'd genuinely believed that McLean was a demon and was about to attack him.

Given the bizarre nature of the crime, no one was surprised when the trial judge accepted the plea of "not criminally responsible." He ordered that Vince Weiguang Li be confined to the Selkirk Mental Health Centre, in Manitoba for an indeterminate time.

That time, as it turned out, would amount to just six years. Li was released on May 8, 2015, a free man after having committed one of Canada's most savage murders.

Death Follows

In the end, it wasn't brilliant detective work but a chicken salad on pumpernickel that ended Robert Durst's life on the run. Durst had been living on the lam for nearly two months, ever since he'd skipped out on a $300,000 bond in Galveston, Texas, a bond that related to the horrific mutilation murder of an elderly man. Now, here he was, shoplifting a $5 sandwich from a Wegmans supermarket in Bethlehem, Pennsylvania and getting himself arrested. All of this while carrying $500 in his pocket and having a further $37,000 in cash stashed in his car. It was just the latest bizarre episode in the life of an extremely unconventional man.

Robert Alan Durst was born in New York City on April 12, 1943. His father was New York real estate mogul Seymour Durst, and Robert and his three younger siblings were raised in a word of affluence and privilege. Not that life in the wealthy enclave of Scarsdale, New York was without trauma. When Robert was just seven years old, his mother committed suicide by jumping from the roof of the family mansion. Robert apparently witnessed the incident and it had a profound effect on him. At age ten, he was diagnosed with "personality decomposition and possible schizophrenia." Whether that diagnosis was accurate or not, he was a loner at school and seemed to shut himself off from other people.

These problems aside, Robert Durst was an intelligent young man who obtained a bachelor's degree in economics from Lehigh University and later enrolled for a Doctorate program at UCLA. However, he dropped out without graduating and returned to New York to work in the family business. That was in 1969, and Robert Durst was living the high life. He rubbed shoulders with the rich and famous, dating Mia Farrow's sister and attending "primal scream" sessions with John Lennon. He was a regular at New York's famous Studio 54 disco; he was friends with Jacqueline Kennedy Onassis; he traveled first-class around the world, sometimes boarding a flight to Europe or Asia on a whim.

But even then, friends described him as an erratic personality. Perhaps that was because of his heavy drug use; or perhaps he was still haunted by the memories of his mother's suicide. Either way, Robert Durst could be a difficult man to get along with, as one impressionable young woman was about to find out.

Durst met Kathleen McCormack in the fall of 1971, when she was a registered nurse with dreams of going back to school and qualifying as a pediatrician. In 1972, she moved into his home in Vermont but soon after Durst's father began pressuring him to move back to New York, to work in the family business. He returned to Manhattan in 1973, bringing Kathleen with him. The couple were married there in April of that year.

At first, the marriage went well. But once Kathleen opted out of her husband's endless round of parties and socializing, the cracks began to appear. Kathleen had good reason for curtailing her social life. She'd registered at the Albert Einstein College of Medicine and was studying towards her degree. That brought a heavy workload but Robert did not seem to understand. It was at around that time that friends started noticing that Kathleen occasionally had bruises on her arms and face. She spoke of divorcing her husband but said that she wouldn't leave without getting what was rightfully hers. A prenuptial agreement made it unlikely that she'd get anything.

And so, the Dursts settled into a kind of truce, moving between the three homes that they owned in New York so that they could avoid ever bumping into each other. Robert was by now dating Prudence Farrow and Kathleen was wrapped up in her studies. She was just a few weeks short of graduating when she disappeared on January 31, 1981.

A friend of Kathleen's had thrown a party in her Manhattan apartment that evening, which Kathleen attended. But she had not been there long, when Durst called, looking for her. Kathleen then spoke to him briefly before telling her friend that she had to leave because her husband was "very upset." She left the party with an ominous message. "If anything happens to me, Bobby did it." It was something told to several of her friends of late.

Four days later, on February 4, 1980, Robert Durst walked into the 20th Precinct, on Manhattan's Upper West side, and reported his wife missing. He said that Kathleen had returned home after the party and that the two of them had gotten into an argument. Eventually, she'd asked him to take her to the Katonah train station where she'd boarded the 9:15 p.m. train back to the city. He hadn't seen or heard from her since. Asked why he'd taken four days to report her missing, Durst said that they lived apart and often went days without seeing each other.

That was all very well but something about Durst's demeanor bothered the detective taking his statement. For a man who had just reported the disappearance of his wife, he was oddly calm. Was it possible that he knew more than he was telling? Initial indications seemed to suggest not. Apparently, Kathleen Durst had called the university on Monday morning to say that she was not feeling well and would have to skip classes. If that was true, then she'd been alive after the Sunday night meeting with her husband.

And yet, Kathleen's friends still believed that Durst was somehow involved in her disappearance. When he offered a $100,000 reward for information about her whereabouts, they saw it as a cynical ploy, designed to cover his tracks. And if that was the case, then he succeeded. Kathleen Durst remains missing to this day and no one has ever been charged in connection with her disappearance. In 1981, Durst filed for divorce from Kathleen, citing spousal abandonment.

Over the next two decades, Robert Durst got back to doing what he'd been doing before his ill-fated marriage to Kathleen. He traveled, he partied, he dated beautiful women and most of all, he made money, lots of it. The Durst Organization had by now grown into a multi-billion-dollar behemoth, one that Robert, as the eldest son, expected to control one day. But those dreams were dealt a death blow in 1994, when Seymour Durst announced that he was stepping down and handing over the reins to his younger son, Douglas. Angered by that decision, Durst quit, setting up business for himself and breaking off all ties with his family.

Robert Durst next appears on our radar in December 2000, when he married his long-time girlfriend, Debrah Charatan, a successful real estate broker. And he shows up again just thirteen days later, when one of his closest friends was found murdered in her Los Angeles home.

Susan Berman had known Durst since they'd studied together at UCLA back in the sixties. Since then, their lives had taken contrasting trajectories. Durst had gone on to become a billionaire through his real estate dealings, Berman had floundered in her chosen career as an author. On December 24, 2000, police were called to Berman's Benedict Canyon home, where they found the 55-year-old lying face down in a pool of blood. A single 9-mm bullet had penetrated the back of her skull.

At first, the consensus was that this was a professional hit. Berman had mob connections. Her father, Davie Berman, had been a partner of Bugsy Siegel in the Flamingo Hotel in Las Vegas and an associate of infamous gangster Meyer Lansky. Susan Berman had, in fact, written two books about her experiences as the daughter of a mobster – Lady Las Vegas and Easy Street. At the time of her death, she was busy scripting a documentary about the Las Vegas mob. Some felt that she had been killed to prevent her revealing secrets that the mob preferred to keep buried.

But the theory didn't really hold up to scrutiny. What could Berman tell that she hadn't already documented in her books? And those books were merely anecdotal. It wasn't as if she'd sat in on high level meetings or been privy to sensitive information. So why would the mob choose to have her killed? The most likely answer was that they wouldn't.

Then the police picked up on something else. Two separate deposits of $25,000 that had been made to Berman's bank account in the weeks leading up to her death. What were these for? Was it possible that she had been blackmailing someone? And if so, who?

Tracking the deposits, investigators found that the check was drawn against real estate magnate, Robert Durst. Durst was, of course, questioned and came up with a viable explanation. Berman, he said, had fallen on hard times. Her books were not selling and a deal to turn her book Easy Street into a movie had fallen through. So too had an option on a play she'd written. Most recently, her ancient sedan had given up the ghost and she'd written to him, asking if she could borrow $7,000 to buy a used car. Durst had done better than that. In November, he'd sent her a check for $25,000, telling her that it was a gift, not a loan. Then, he'd decided that $25,000 was not enough and had doubled it.

The LAPD were suspicious of Durst's story. They had already noted that he'd been in California when Berman was killed and had flown out the morning after. They'd also formed the opinion that Susan Berman had been killed by someone she knew. Berman, according to those who knew her, was a notoriously jittery person. She would not have allowed a stranger into her home. And she'd been shot in the back of the head, which meant that she'd turned her back on the killer. That could only indicate that she knew and trusted the shooter. Further investigation revealed that Berman had been contacted by the New York State Police just a few weeks before her death. They wanted to speak to her about the 1982 disappearance of Kathleen Durst.

And what might Berman have known about that? Was it possible that Robert Durst had told her something? Was it possible, as some of Kathleen's friends believed, that it had been Berman who'd phoned the medical school on the day after Kathleen went missing, pretending to be Kathleen? Had she been using that knowledge to extort money from her old friend? We may never know the answer to those questions. What we do know is that just days before she was killed, Berman told a friend that she had information that was going to "blow the top off things." It was information that she never got the chance to share. Durst in any case, had dropped out of sight. When officers tried to question him again about the Berman murder, he was nowhere to be found.

On September 30, 2001, nine months after the murder of Susan Berman, and a million miles from the bright lights of New York and L.A., a 13-year-old boy was fishing near his home in Galveston,

Texas. Spotting something in the water, he called to his father, who initially thought that the object was a dead pig. Closer inspection proved it to be a human torso with the head and limbs hacked off.

That same day, another fisherman reported seeing trash bags floating in with the tide. When police hauled these ashore and opened them up, they were found to contain the arms and legs that belonged to the torso. The head, however, was still missing and was never found. Not that it was needed for identification purposes, the fingers were intact and the prints produced a match to a man named Morris Black, who had a minor misdemeanor on file.

By all accounts, 71-year-old Morris Black was a cranky old-timer, a loner who lived in a four-unit apartment building at 2213 Avenue K in Galveston. Known for his quick temper and somewhat cantankerous nature, Black could nonetheless be charitable when the mood took him. He'd once bid on five cases of reading glasses on an Internet auction and had donated them to a local charity with the stipulation that they be given away to the needy.

Calling at the apartment building that was Black's last known address, detectives learned that he'd lived in one of the two upper floor apartments. The other unit was occupied by a middle-aged woman named Dorothy Ciner. According to the landlord, Ciner suffered from a debilitating throat condition and communicated only through written notes. She lived alone but sometimes had a visit from a male friend.

Having gleaned this information from the landlord, the detectives went upstairs and immediately noticed a trail of blood leading from Black's apartment to Ciner's. When knocking at Ciner's door brought no response, the police entered, using a passkey provided by the landlord. They then searched the apartment and found a pair of blood-encrusted boots and a bloody knife. There were also traces of blood on the kitchen floor, the carpets and the apartment door. Of Dorothy Ciner, however, there was no trace. It appeared, she'd flown the coop.

The police were not without clues, though. Ciner had provided the license plate number of her Honda CRV on her lease application. When they ran it through the Division of Motor Vehicles database, they were in for a surprise. The vehicle was registered to Robert Durst.

Nine days after Morris Black's body had been pulled from the water, a Galveston patrolman spotted Durst's silver Honda and set off in pursuit. Durst made no effort to escape or to deny his true identity. He was arrested at the scene and later charged with the murder of Morris Black. Bail was set at $300,000, a pittance for a man like Durst. It was quickly posted by his wife Debrah Charatan. Then Durst disappeared once more.

Robert Durst would remain at large for 44 days, during which he traveled to Dallas, New Orleans, Connecticut and New York, before ending up in Pennsylvania. In New Orleans, he'd used his old ruse, dressing up as a woman and claiming to be mute, this time using the name, "Dianne Winn." Who knows how long he would have remained at large had he not pulled that ill-advised theft of the chicken sandwich.

Durst was extradited to Texas on January 28, 2002. At his arraignment he admitted killing Morris Black, but claimed that he had acted in self-defense, after Black attacked him. Given the severe injuries inflicted on Black, that appeared a foolhardy strategy but in the end it worked. Durst's assertion was that his gun had accidentally discharged during a struggle for control of the weapon. The bullet had struck Black in the face, killing him instantly. Durst had then decided to dismember the body, using an axe and several saws for that purpose. Since Black's head had never been recovered, it was impossible for the prosecutor to disprove accidental shooting. The jury therefore acquitted Durst of murder, although he was found guilty of evidence tampering. He was sentenced to five years in prison and paroled in 2005, after serving three.

Durst's legal problems however, are far from over. On Monday, November 7, 2016, he was arraigned in Los Angeles for the murder of Susan Berman. If found guilty on that charge, he could face a possible death sentence. Police in Vermont and California are also investigating the disappearances of three teenagers, all of them in some way connected with Robert Durst. Additionally, the FBI has formed a task team to look at cold cases in jurisdictions where Durst is known to have lived, often under false identities. These include Vermont, New York, California, Massachusetts, New Jersey, South Carolina, Florida, Texas, Mississippi, and Virginia. It seems that everywhere Robert Durst went, death followed.

For more True Crime books by Robert Keller
please visit:
http://bit.ly/kellerbooks

Made in the USA
Middletown, DE
08 December 2017